Lingerie design on the Stand

DESIGNS FOR UNDERWEAR AND NIGHTWEAR

dawn cloake

B.T.BATSFORD LTD, LONDON

Dedication

For my parents, William and Mary Driscoll, with loving memories. My father's love of classical prose and poetry and his ability to speak and write eloquently on many subjects has always been my inspiration and my mother's loving patience and devotion to duty the example to follow when completing difficult tasks.

Acknowledgements

I am grateful to the following people who continue to offer me their support in various ways:

To Business Manager Alanah Cullen and her staff of the D.A.L.I. (Developments at London College of Fashion) Professional Development Unit at London College of Fashion, for their continued interest and support.

To Nina Spanovangelis, for sharing her idea of modelling fabric over a grapefruit to demonstrate to beginners the intricacies of shaping fabric to the bust curves and for permission to use it in this book; also for promoting my books through her work here in the UK and at The National Institute of Fashion Technology (NIFT) on programs under the auspices of the United Nations Development Projects (UNDP) currently funded by the Ministry of Textiles, Government of India

To Kennett and Lindsell, the garment stand manufacturers, for the continued loan of the dress stand with legs, which enables me to experiment freely and to develop different kinds of blocks useful to both modellers and flat pattern cutters, such as the nether region and bra blocks in this book.

To my husband, for his unfailing advice, critical judgement and encouragement, and to Simon Rosenheim, Art Director and his staff at B. T. Batsford, London for their continued interest in publishing my work.

Last, but constantly at the forefront of my thoughts, is my gratitude for the very existence of The Royal London Homoeopathic Hospital in Great Ormond Street, London and its learned and dedicated staff, particularly Dr Marysia Kratimenos, Consultant Dr Peter Fisher and Mr Tariq Khan of the Marigold Clinic for putting me 'back on my own two feet' and making sure I stay that way.

First published 2000
© Dawn Cloake 2000

Illustrations by Dawn Cloake

ISBN 0 7134 8552 3

A CIP catalogue record for this book is available from the British Library.

Printed in Spain
for the publishers,
B. T. Batsford Ltd,
9 Blenheim Court,
Brewery Road,
London N7 9NT

A member of the Chrysalis Group plc

Contents

Introduction   4
Equipment for patternmaking   **6**
Taking measurements   10
Lingerie fabrics and accessories   14
Introductory or refresher modelling techniques   16

Underwear Section   **29**
Bras   29
Bodies and support pants   40
Tights   45
Briefs, slips and camisoles   46

Nightwear Section   **60**
Nightdresses and negligees   60
Robes and pyjamas   68
Mules   80

Underwear as eveningwear   **82**
Body beneath the suit   82
Waspie or evening cummerband?   83
Bustiers   84
Little black vest   85
Evening shift   86
Camisoles   87
Lace evening coat and trousers   88
Embroidered stockings or tights   89

Blocks   **90**
Padded Arm   90
Bra and Gusset Blocks   92

Glossary   **94**
Suppliers list and further reading   **95**
Index   **96**

Introduction

Lingerie Design on the Stand is a sequel to *Fashion Design on the Stand*, which provided a systematic course of instruction for the modelling and draping of day and eveningwear garments. Teachers, students, designers and pattern makers in industry have been searching for a similar reference work for creating patterns for all types of underwear and nightwear. Very little has been written on the subject of making patterns for this section of the clothing market, although the production of these garments accounts for large sections of clothing industries. This book includes some flat pattern cutting but the emphasis is on the designer's tool - the garment stand - where fabric characteristics exert their own influence and play a strong part in the designer's final creation.

This book is intended for students and teachers involved in pattern making in fashion and art colleges and schools, for practising designers in the clothing industry and for individual designers and dressmakers working in small workrooms or from home. The book is divided into two broad sections covering underwear and nightwear, then further sub-divided into close-fitting foundation (next to the skin) garments such as bras, 'bodies' and boned and underwired bras, followed by briefs, slips, camisoles and tights. Nightwear is divided into nightdresses and negligees, pyjamas and robes, with a special collection of mix 'n match nightwear for students living away from home, fun pyjama tops and bottoms, tabards, jerkins, robes and mules which can be worn outside the bedroom. The book ends with examples of underwear as eveningwear: sequinned and metallic embroidered tops, organdie camisoles, a 'body' beneath a suit by day becomes an evening top, embroidered stockings worn with a leather mini-skirt and boots, a night 'shift', and includes an outfit in sheer fabric and lace which would be equally suitable for evening entertaining or the bedroom.

The modelling exercises have been selected to introduce the reader to a variety of techniques which can be used in day and eveningwear as well as lingerie, including kimono, raglan, dropped shoulder sleeves, strap-front openings and other processes. Woven and non-woven fabrics, with and without the stretch factor, have been used to provide different 'handling' experiences plus a variety of techniques for introducing the extra movement needed in nightwear, such as the modelling of gathers into yokes, insertion of tucks and the construction of flared styles.

Pattern making for lingerie and nightwear involves two quite different modelling techniques, a very close fit for 'foundation' garments such as bras, briefs and 'bodies' and a very loose fit in nightwear to allow for movement during sleep. Between these come the 'normal' fit for garments such as slips, panties and camisoles, which require tolerance for movement when using woven fabrics and the removal of some, or all, tolerance when using stretch fabrics. The book has been designed to incorporate all these factors in an uncomplicated way by grouping together garments which require similar solutions. For instance all nether garments (those with a division between the legs) appear together in the underwear section. The exception to this is the pyjama trouser, which can be found in the nightwear section.

Any garments involving a division of the skirt to create openings for the legs are more easily modelled on a stand with legs. The professional lingerie workroom, even if producing patterns by the flat cutting method, would be expected to invest in at least one such stand, if only for evaluating toiles. However, for those who do not possess this type of stand and who are restricted to the 'torso' length stand which is cut off horizontally at 40cm (16") below the waistline, a full-size pattern for the hip to upper thigh section of the dress stand has been included (page7).

Garments can be modelled down to hip level, removed from the stand and the pattern used to complete shaping below the hipline. The size chart on pages 12-13 is in both metric and imperial measurements and includes a column showing the amount of tolerance required for normal body movement in daywear garments and the stand (or block) measurement. A shorter, 'Lingerie measurement' chart can be found on page 28 for determining bra and bra-cup size.

Historically, underwear was made of linen, later of calico and was hidden beneath outer garments, but some garments, such as the bra, vest, camisole and slip have recently evolved as both day and eveningwear. Some examples of this transition can be seen in 'Underwear as eveningwear' in luxury fabrics designed to be seen, and include a sequinned camisole, day and evening 'shifts' and a lace coat with matching trousers and alternative pleated sheer fabric trousers.

The term 'lingerie' has always conjured up images of beautiful garments cleverly cut on the bias and made up in delicate fabrics trimmed with exquisite laces and ribbons. Lingerie occupies its own special corner of the undergarment section of the clothing industry and attracts designers who love to handle such fabrics and create garments of great beauty. The subject of pattern-making for underwear and nightwear is vast and demands different approaches to design and pattern construction. Within the clothing industry there are distinct dividing lines between foundationwear (corsetry) comprising skin-tight garments such as bras, bodies and suspender belts; underwear (slips, camisoles and briefs) and nightwear (pyjamas, nightdresses and robes). This

book is intended as an introduction to modelling patterns for these three sections. Patterns for lingerie and nightwear may be constructed by two-dimensional flat cutting on paper or by three-dimensional modelling with fabric directly on the stand. The choice of modelling designs directly on the stand is deliberate. Stands designed for lingerie and swimwear closely resemble the human body and familiarise the designer with the body shape beneath the garment.

The book begins with skin-tight styles where no extra tolerance for body movement is needed in the garment, progressing to second layer styles such as slips and panties requiring some tolerance, followed by nightdresses and pyjamas which need exaggerated amounts of tolerance. The intention is to offer a variety of modelling experiences to familiarise students and designers with the shape of the body and the need for different tolerance requirements for garments. Students on most pattern-making courses work mainly with flat pattern cutting and many find difficulty in constructing two-dimensional patterns to fit a three-dimensional body. It is suggested that working directly on the dress stand leads to greater understanding of the three-dimensional nature of the body and should precede, or be studied simultaneously with the more abstract method of flat pattern cutting.

Equipment for patternmaking

Garment stand: also known as 'form' or 'model'. Special stands are available for different types of garment, including dresses, skirts, trousers, lingerie and swimwear.

Modelling fabric (for making toiles): unbleached calico, muslin or or any other inexpensive fabric which resembles the weight of the garment to be modelled.

Shears: for cutting fabric and small, very sharp scissors for snipping into seam allowances; scissors for cutting paper and card.

Pins: long, fine pins are available for modelling fine fabrics. 'Lills' (very short pins) are useful for taping design lines on the stand. They sink into the surface at an angle, and are easily removed by pulling the tape off the stand. A pin-cushion strapped to the wrist enables both hands to hold fabric in position on the stand during modelling.

Needle & thread: for tacking up toiles.

Narrow black stay tape (width 7mm): for taping design lines on the stand

Tape and metre rule measure: with both metric and imperial measures. Short ruler.

Set square: essential for obtaining right angles on patterns and fabrics.

Tracing wheel: for copying patterns and for transferring lines from modelled fabric.

French curve: useful for drawing smooth neck and armhole and curved seams.

Pencils: hard pencils are marked with an H and produce fine, clear lines for pattern making. Soft pencils, marked HB are best for drawing and marking fabric.

Pattern paper: for creating patterns from the modelled toiles and for developing some designs by 'flat pattern cutting'. The paper may be plain, graph, or printed with 'dot and cross' marks which provide a guide for right-angles and straight lines. Fine, clear, flexible plastic can be used for smooth areas but has no grain and will not drape.

Mirror: a full-length mirror placed behind the stand or live model enables the designer to judge the all-round effect of the garment.

Other useful items: weights, which hold down fabric, card or paper patterns and prevent their moving when being outlined, a stiletto or 'scriber' for puncturing small holes in card, and a notcher, which clips out a small narrow rectangle (a 'notch') in fabric, blocks or patterns. Notebook and file for recording exercises.

Half-scale size 12 block: for right-hand side front and back nether region from high hip level, 10cm (4") below waistline to upper thigh. The block has been modelled on a size 12 legged stand and is intended for patternmakers who wish to model garments with legs but who only have access to a torso stand with no legs. Photocopy or draft the block to twice its size, then trace off the front and back sections separately. Adjust the block to the garment being modelled. Surplus fabric at the back thigh may be elasticated. Grade as for any other block. The dotted line represents the back, the solid line the front. No seam allowance has been added.

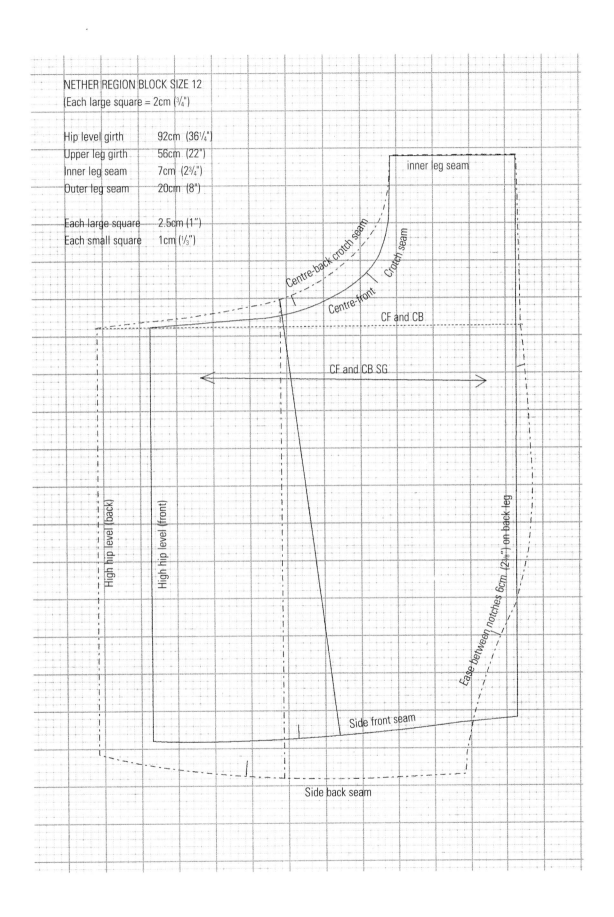

NETHER REGION BLOCK SIZE 12
(Each large square = 2cm (³/₄"))

Hip level girth   92cm (36¼")
Upper leg girth   56cm (22")
Inner leg seam   7cm (2³/₄")
Outer leg seam   20cm (8")

Each large square   2.5cm (1")
Each small square   1cm (¹/₃")

inner leg seam

Centre-back crotch seam

Crotch seam

Centre-front

CF and CB

CF and CB SG

High hip level (back)

High hip level (front)

Ease between notches 6cm (2¹/₈") on back leg

Side front seam

Side back seam

Lingerie stands

Dress stands are usually 'torso' length, reach to well below the hip line and represent the figure with foundationwear and undergarments, such as a slip, as a foundation for modelling and fitting daywear. Such stands may be used in lingerie and nightwear design for camisoles, waist-length and full-length slips, nightdresses and robes. Very close-fitting garments such as bras require further adjustment to tighten the fit in the same way that close-fitting boned bodices and bustiers need extra tightening to hug the figure. Strictly speaking, bras and other close-fitting foundation garments come under the heading of corsetry, but will be modelled with other lingerie items in this book.

'Nether' garments, those with a division between the legs, such as panties, 'bodies', camiknickers and pyjama trousers need a stand with legs and designers specialising in nether garments have a variety of suitable stands from which to choose. However, most designers, teachers and students are more likely to have access to a torso daywear stand than a lingerie stand with legs, so the instructions in this book will include the adjustments to be made to the final pattern if stands other than the lingerie stand are used. In

addition, for those readers who have access only to a torso stand, trace off the block (basic pattern) of the hip to thigh area on page 7. Use this in the same way as other pattern cutting blocks to develop the lower part of the garment. The upper part of 'bodies' and camiknickers can be modelled and the lower part produced by flat pattern cutting. Trouser blocks in any size required can also be adapted to make the lower part of underwear and pyjamas.

The diagrams opposite show the main differences between the stands. For the serious lingerie designer, the acquisition of a stand designed specifically to follow the curves of the unclothed body is obviously a great advantage. No further adjustments to the modelled toiles are needed. Learning to adjust patterns made on a torso stand, however, provides opportunities for students to increase their knowledge and understanding of the body shape and of the modelling and flat pattern cutting techniques needed to do this.

The sketches below show how the block on page 7 fits the figure when assembled. The back leg needs to be elasticated. Otherwise the pattern fits exactly. Use it like any other block, reducing its size for stretch fabrics and increasing it for loose garments. The pattern was modelled on a size 12 legged stand and the grading increment to smaller or larger sizes is 5cm (2") per size. (See 'increments' in last column of size chart on pages 12-13)

NETHER REGION BLOCK

How the block exactly fits the figure

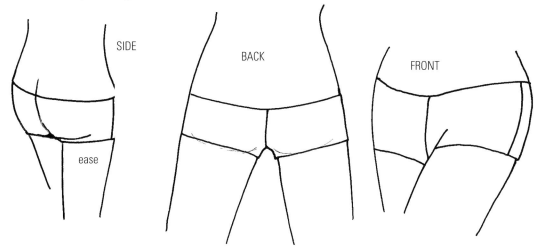

(a) The torso length dress stand is suitable for modelling dresses, blouses and skirts, evening and partywear, but requires adjustment to the final pattern for low necklines, sleeveless styles and foundationwear. Note the smooth shape of the stand, with little reference to the true contours of the breasts and buttocks or hollows at front armhole.

(b) The full length lingerie stand with legs has contours more closely shaped to the un-clothed figure. It is suitable for foundation, lingerie and swimwear. Note the more pronounced shape of breasts, cleavage gap and hollows between the arm and the chest. The buttocks are also more realistically shaped. However, it is difficult to manipulate the fabric between the legs, which are rigid. A half-stand is indispensable for perfecting the inner groin area of nether garments (d).

(c) The trouser stand starts above the waistline, reaches the ankle and is suitable for panties, shorts, trousers and pyjamas.

(d) Half-trouser stand with easier access to obtaining the correct shape for the crotch area.

* *When ordering from manufacturers, be careful to specify which type of stand is required - daywear, outerwear, lingerie or swimwear.*

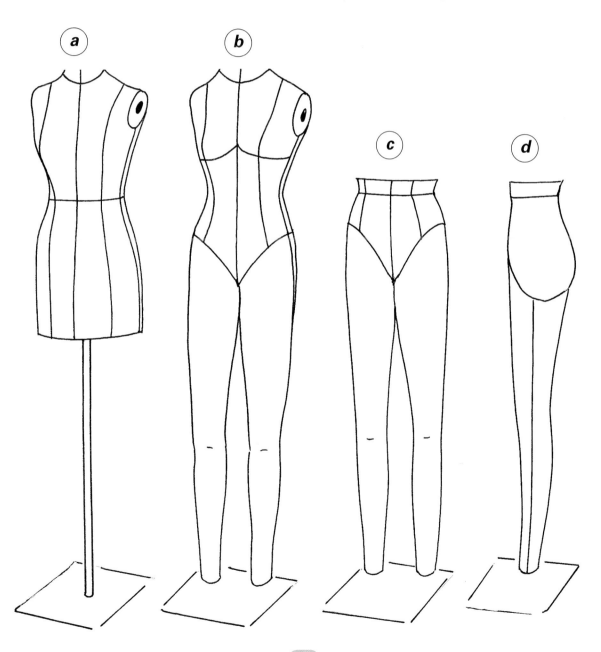

Taking measurements ('girth' = circumference)

It is convenient when measuring the figure to take all horizontal measurements first,
working from head to foot; then take the vertical measurements. The list below includes some
measurements not found in standard charts but which are useful check measures.

Horizontal

1	Neck girth	Round base of neck
2	Shoulder length	From side of neck to bone at end of shoulder
3	Across shoulders	Between ends of shoulder bones at back and front
4	Across back	About 10.5cm (4 1/8 ") below nape
5	Across chest	About 10cm (4") below base of front neck
6	Underarm level	Keep tape horizontal round back & front underarm level
7	Over bust girth	Round body, under the arms but above the bust
8	Bust level girth	Round fullest part of bust, tape horizontal at back
9	Under bust girth	Round rib cage under bust
10	Bust separation	Between the nipples in a straight line
11	*Armhole girth	Girth between shoulder ends via underarm
12	Waistline	Round narrowest part of waist
13	High hip line	About 10cm (4") below waistline
14	Hip, widest part	Round fullest part of hip about 20cm (8") from waistline
15	Bicep (top arm)	Round fullest part of top arm muscle
16	Elbow	Round slightly bent arm
17	Wrist	Round wrist at wristbone
18	Thigh	Round widest part of leg between groin and knee
19	Knee	Round mid-knee
20	Calf	Widest part between knee and ankle
21	Ankle	Round ankle at bone

Vertical

22	Full height	From top of head to floor without shoes
23	Nape to back waist	From nape (bump at back neck) to waist level
24	Nape to floor	From nape to floor level
25	Waist to hip	Waist level to hip level
26	Waist to knee	Waist level to mid-knee
27	Waist to floor	Waist level to floor
28	Outer sleeve	From shoulder-end to wrist, arm slightly bent
29	Body rise	Seated, from waist-level to flat surface
30	Crotch length	From centre-front to centre-back waist through legs
31	Nape to nipple	From nape over shoulder to nipple

* The armhole girth is difficult to measure on the figure. Consult the measurement chart for nearest standard measurement.

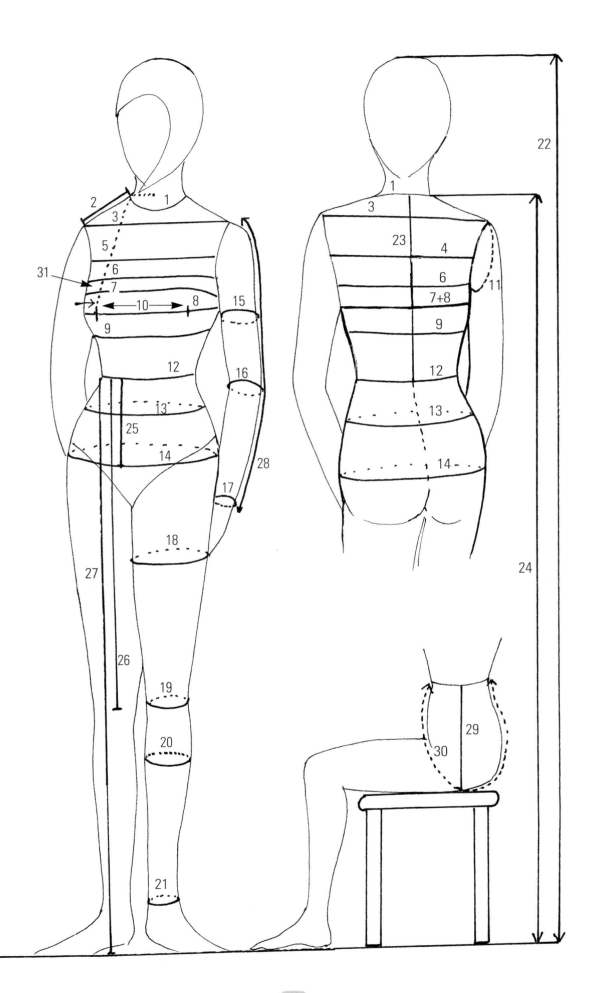

Size charts

The following measurements represent body size, not block or stand size. The figures shown in the 'Body tolerance' column refer to the amounts already incorporated in the stand or flat cutting blocks to allow for normal body movement for daywear garments. It is these amounts which will be changed when modelling close-fitting foundationwear or loose nightwear.

Standard chart measurements vary from one book, college or manufacturer to another and most charts do not indicate what tolerances for body movement have been included. What should remain standard is the increments between the sizes - 5cm (2") shown in the last column. It is necessary to check the size of the stand or block being used and to understand where and how much tolerance is required to produce well-fitting and comfortable garments. This information can be found with the individual exercises throughout the book.

METRIC AND IMPERIAL STANDARD MEASUREMENT CHART FOR WOMEN OF MEDIUM HEIGHT 160-170cm (5′ 3" - 5′ 7")

Size	8	10	12	14	16	18	Body tolerance	Total size 12	Increment
Neck	34	35	36	37	38	39	-	36	1.0
	13³⁄₈"	13³⁄₄"	14¹⁄₈"	14¹⁄₂"	15"	15³⁄₈"	-	14¹⁄₈"	³⁄₈"
Shoulder	11.5	11.7	11.9	12.1	12.3	12.5	-	11.9	1.0
	4¹⁄₂"	4⁵⁄₈"	4³⁄₄"	4⁷⁄₈"	4⁷⁄₈"	5"	-	4⁷⁄₈"	³⁄₈"
Across back	34.0	35.0	36.0	37.0	38.0	39.0	1.6	37.6	1.2
	13³⁄₈"	13³⁄₄"	14¹⁄₈"	14¹⁄₂"	15"	15³⁄₈"	⁵⁄₈"	14¹⁄₂"	¹⁄₂"
Across chest	31.5	32.5	33.5	34.5	35.5	36.5	0.6	34.1	1.2
	12³⁄₈"	13"	13¹⁄₈"	13¹⁄₂"	14"	14³⁄₈"	¹⁄₄"	13³⁄₈"	¹⁄₂"
Underarm level	74.0	78.0	82.0	86.0	90.0	94.0	-	82.0	-
	29¹⁄₈"	30³⁄₄"	32¹⁄₄"	33⁷⁄₈"	35¹⁄₂"	37"	-	32¹⁄₄"	-
Bust	80.0	84.0	88	93.0	98.0	103.0	10.0	98.0	5.0
	31¹⁄₂"	33"	34⁵⁄₈"	36⁵⁄₈"	38⁵⁄₈"	40¹⁄₂"	4"	38⁵⁄₈"	2"
Bust separation	16.8	18.0	19.2	20.4	21.6	22.8	-	19.2	1.2
	6⁵⁄₈"	7¹⁄₈"	7¹⁄₂"	8"	8¹⁄₂"	9"	-	7¹⁄₂"	¹⁄₂"
Rib cage	61.0	66.0	71.0	76.0	81.0	86.0	-	71.0	5.0
	24"	26"	28"	30"	32"	34"	-	28"	2"
Waist	60.0	64.0	68.0	72.0	76.0	80.0	Skirts 1(³⁄₈")	69.0(27¹⁄₈")	5.0
							Trousers 1(³⁄₈")	69.0(27¹⁄₈")	
							Dresses 4(1⁵⁄₈")	72.0(28³⁄₈")	
	23⁵⁄₈"	25¹⁄₈"	26³⁄₄"	28³⁄₈"	30"	31¹⁄₂"	-		2"
High hip	80.0	84.0	88.0	92.0	96.0	100.0	4-5	92	5.0
	31¹⁄₂"	33"	34⁵⁄₈"	36⁵⁄₈"	38⁵⁄₈"	40¹⁄₂"	1³⁄₄"	36¹⁄₄"	2"
Hip	86.0	90.0	94.0	98.0	102.0	106.0	5.0	99.0	5.0
	33⁷⁄₈"	35¹⁄₂"	37"	38⁵⁄₈"	40¹⁄₈"	41³⁄₄"	2"	39"	2"
Thigh	48.8	51.0	54.0	57.0	60.0	63	-	54	3.2
	19¹⁄₄"	20"	21¹⁄₄"	22³⁄₈"	23⁵⁄₈"	24³⁄₄"	-	21¹⁄₄"	1¹⁄₄"
Knee	32.2	33.6	35	36.4	37.8	39.2	6	41	1.4
	12⁵⁄₈"	13¹⁄₄"	13³⁄₄"	14³⁄₈"	14⁷⁄₈"	15¹⁄₂"	2³⁄₈"	16¹⁄₈"	¹⁄₂"
Calf	30.2	31.6	33	34.4	35.8	37.2	-	33	1.4
	11⁷⁄₈"	12¹⁄₂"	13"	13¹⁄₂"	14"	14⁵⁄₈"	-	13"	¹⁄₂"
Ankle	21.8	22.4	23	23.6	24.2	24.8	9	32	0.7
	8⁵⁄₈"	8⁷⁄₈"	9"	9¹⁄₄"	9¹⁄₂"	9³⁄₄"	3¹⁄₂"	12¹⁄₂"	¹⁄₄"

Size	8	10	12	14	16	18	Body tolerance	Total size 12	Increment
Outer sleeve	56.2	57.1	58.0	58.9	59.8	60.7	-	58	0.9
	22⅛"	22½"	22⅞"	23⅛"	23½"	23⅞"	-	22⅞"	⅜"
Armhole	38.6	40.0	42.6	44.6	46.6	48.6	-	42.6	2.0
	15¼"	15¾"	16¾"	17½"	18⅜"	19⅛"	-	16¾"	¾"
Bicep	22.9	24.7	26.5	28.3	30.1	31.9	5	31.5	1.8
	9"	9¾"	10½"	11⅛"	11⅞"	12½"	2"	12½"	¾"
Elbow	22.2	23.6	25.0	26.4	27.8	29.2	5	30.0	1.8
	8¾"	9⅜"	9⅞"	10⅜"	11"	11½"	2"	11⅞"	¾"
Wrist	15.0	15.5	16.0	16.5	17.0	17.5	6.5	22.5	0.8
	5⅞"	6⅛"	6¼"	6½"	6¾"	6⅞"	2½"	8¾"	⅜"
Nape to back waist	40.0	40.5	41.0	41.5	42.0	42.5	-	41	0.6
	15¾"	16"	16⅛"	16⅜"	16½"	16¾"	-	16⅛"	¼"
Waist to hip	19.4	19.7	20.0	20.3	20.6	20.9	-	20	0.3
	7⅝"	7¾"	7⅞"	8"	8⅛"	8¼"	-	7⅞"	⅛"
Waist to knee	58.4	59.2	60.0	60.8	61.6	62.4	-	60	0.9
	23"	23⅜"	23⅝"	24"	24¼"	24½"	-	23⅝"	⅜"
Waist to floor	100.4	101.7	103	104.3	105.6	106.9	-	103	1.8
	39½"	40"	40½"	41"	41½"	42"	-	40½"	¾"
Nape to nipple	33.5	34.0	34.5	35.0	35.5	36.0	-	34.5	1.4
	13⅛"	13⅜"	13½"	13¾"	14"	14⅛"	-	13½"	½"
Body rise (crotch depth)	26.4	27.2	28.0	28.8	29.6	30.4	Included due to seat position	28.0	1.1
	10⅜"	10¾"	11"	11⅜"	11⅝"	12"		11"	½"
Crotch length	61.0	63.5	66.0	68.5	71.0	73.5	Varies with style	66.0	2.5
	24"	25"	26"	27"	28"	29"	-	26"	1"

Lingerie fabrics and accessories

The development of a wide range of stretch fabrics for foundation garments, those worn next to the skin, has allowed lingerie designers to move away from the traditional pattern-making techniques used in woven fabrics. Corsets, with boned panels and extra bands of straight grain fabric to control stomach and bust to give a firmer line have now been replaced to a large extent by stretch 'bodies'. Underwiring or lightweight stretch fabric now replace the firm double fabric rib-cage band which kept bra cups in place.

Stretch fabrics, mainly knitted, have played a part in bra design for many years and fine but strong lingerie elastic has largely replaced tape and ribbon in maintaining a firm edge and close fit, although where a very firm edge is necessary, as in larger sizes, ribbon can be used effectively to provide extra support. It is now possible to purchase many elastomeric fabrics which are suitable for the bra cups. The fabrics are very flexible in all directions and can be moulded over the cup and kept in position by the firm outer design edge which is necessary to prevent 'riding up'. Short plastic bones are often inserted at the side of the bust or the seam otherwise firmed to keep the fabric taut.

Bra straps perform a similar task to the shoulder seams of other garments. They keep the garment in position, support its weight and the weight of the bust.

Strong, soft-backed lingerie elastic in various widths can be used as shoulder straps stitched onto the front and back of the bra. Sometimes looped through small metal rings attached to the bra by a separate ribbon loop which tended to tear off in wear, it is now more usual to find that the design of the upper bra cup includes a self-fabric loop which encircles a metal ring or buckle through which the strap is slotted. The straps are cut longer than the body measurement needed, and include a device for adjusting the strap length for personal body size and comfort. Bra straps can be extended to join ready-made hooks and loops and can be ordered to match fabrics.

Bra accessories

Foundation garments must be comfortable and fit well. In this the designer's choice of fabric is crucial. Comfort includes the choice of natural or synthetic fibres or combinations of these to suit different requirements. The addition of Lycra and other synthetic elastomeric fibres to many lingerie fabrics gives a degree of stretch which helps designers and pattern makers to create well-fitting, comfortable garments without recourse to the darts, gathers and tucks necessary to control surplus material in woven fabrics.

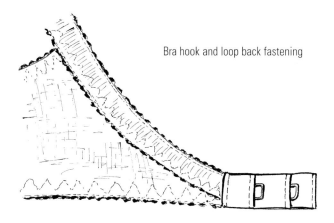

Bra hook and loop back fastening

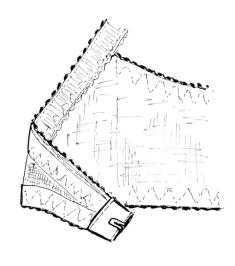

Underwires and cup dividers

Underwiring is frequently used for the lower part of the bra cup to support the bust and control the garment shape on the body. The diagram below shows the shape of underwiring and its position in the bra. The lower half of the bust circle is the guide for underwiring and is taped onto the stand or incorporated into advanced pattern-making blocks for reference purposes. See page 31 for drawing the bust circle onto the stand. An underwire is based on a semicircle of steel with plastic protectors at each end to prevent penetration of the fabric and damage to the skin. The underarm side is longer than centre front (see diagram below). Underwires support the bust and prevent the bra riding up. They require a casing, often simply a narrow tape or ribbon, and can be inserted during the last stages of sewing the bra. A cup divider maintains the centre front division between two bra cups and keeps the bra in shape against the skin. Padded cups and half cups may also be inserted into a bra and are described under 'Padding the stand' on page 21.

Bras for sportswear

Except for very small sizes, most women still need a bra to support the bust during vigorous activity such as competitive sports and manufacturers have developed elastomeric bras in a large range of sizes to give smooth but firm support to the sportswoman. Using stretch fabrics removes the need for darts and seams with drastic curves to fit the bust and helps to achieve

a smooth fit under close-fitting garments. It is also possible to eliminate all seams and darts by using a heat process to permanently stretch the centre of a circle of fabric, producing the no-seam bra.

Fabric and the garment stand

'Modelling' and 'draping' are terms used to describe the way in which fabric is applied to the dress stand or the human body in the creation of garment designs. Although the terms are interchangeable, 'modelling' more aptly describes smoothing, shaping and cutting fabric to define the body contours and controlling the shape with darts and seamlines, while 'draping' suggests the artistic arrangement of folds (hence 'drapes') which float across the form with fewer controls (seams and darts). In both techniques, the essential factor is the understanding of the fabric, its weight, texture, hang and draping qualities.

This book is concerned mainly with modelling and draping fabrics suitable for lingerie and nightwear - natural and man-made, woven, knitted, elastomeric and netted fabrics. Lingerie and nightwear include very close, 'skin-tight' garments such as bras and 'bodies' and very loose garments such as nightdresses and pyjamas and employ different types of handling techniques.

The techniques of modelling and draping used to take place on the human figure, and live models are still used in some establishments, usually for the later stages in the design process when the garment can be

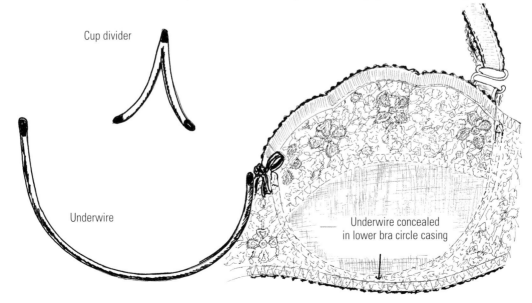

Cup divider

Underwire

Underwire concealed
in lower bra circle casing

evaluated more realistically on the human figure. Even the best dress stands are poor substitutes for the human form. They cannot sit, bend or stretch and have no arms. Detachable arms are stiff and do not bend at the elbow. Manufacturers give very little information in their catalogues to potential purchasers. Usually the most known about the stand is its standard size and shape, i.e., torso stand, stand with legs, lingerie or skirt stand. Stands of the same size vary according to the age, stage of development and physique of the average person they represent and may be taller or shorter, have a longer or shorter nape to waist length and a higher or lower bust level. The designer and pattern maker need to work out the exact size of the stand to determine how much, if any, body tolerance has been added (See page 19).

Dress stands have more than one function. They are part of the design process for modelling and draping new designs; they are also used for evaluating the toile (trial garment) and for appraising the final garment in both modelling and flat pattern cutting and as an aid to designing or testing sections of a garment such as determining the depth of a neckline or creating a shoulder drape.

For modelling garments a strong stand on a heavy base is essential. Lightweight, expandable stands, although useful to home dressmakers, are unsuitable for constant use in a design room. Once expanded to a larger size, the gaps which occur at the stand seamlines make it impossible to determine the exact centre-front and back, the true shoulder or waist line and essential body measurements such as bust separation.

Note: *A pattern for a flexible padded arm can be found on page 90.*

Introductory or refresher modelling techniques

If you are new to designing on the dress stand, or need a refresher, the information and exercises in this section will teach you the basic techniques of modelling before you attempt the lingerie and nightwear designs. You will learn how to measure and tape the dress stand, understand the fabric grain, shape fabric to the curves of the stand and to manipulate surplus fabric into darts and shaped seams.

In this section the following basic modelling techniques will be covered:
1. Determining stand size
2. Padding the stand
3. Taping essential body positions
4. Taping design lines
5. Understanding fabric grain
6. Preparing the fabric for a design
7. Controlling the fabric grain vertically and horizontally on the stand
8. Shaping woven fabric to curves by creating darts

1. Determining stand size

In the British Clothing Industry most womens' garment designs for production are first modelled (or cut by flat pattern cutting) to size 12, then graded to other sizes. Size 12 is also the recognised standard size for use in teaching and most colleges have a predominance of size 12 dress stands and block patterns. The exercises in this book will follow this tradition, but references will be made to other sizes where appropriate and the body tolerances for UK sizes 8-18 (USA sizes 6-16) are included in the size chart on pages 12-13. The amounts of tolerance added to pattern cutting blocks and dress stands vary from country to country. The amounts listed in this chart give a close fit but allow normal body movement such as bending, stretching and sitting.

Garments are made to the following measurements:

Body size plus body tolerance for normal movement, plus 'ease' where necessary, such as the sleevehead for a set-in sleeve, plus 'designer ease' where appropriate, when a garment's style requires extra fabric to achieve the determined shape. Sportswear is now made mainly from stretch fabrics but requires more body tolerance for active movement than normal daywear. Close-fitting eveningwear and foundation garments require less tolerance. Stretch fabric may have some or all tolerance removed for all types of close-fitting clothing. However, fabric with the 'stretch factor' is now used in looser garments and the designer and pattern cutter need to be aware of the constant changes in fabric characteristics.

Compare the body size (standard or individual) to stand size.

The chart indicates how to record this information. The same amounts of tolerance apply to other sizes.

Insert the measurements of the dress stand being used in column five. In the last column, insert the difference between the amount in the 'Total' column and the 'Dress stand' column. This is the minimum amount to add when pattern-making and will give a close fit plus sufficient room not to strain garment seams during normal movements.

For other measurements refer to the size charts on pages 12-13. Illustrations on page 19 show positions for taking horizontal measurement on the stand and the live model. The amounts in the 'tolerance' column below should be added to these.

Area	Body size 12 (from size chart or individual)	Plus tolerance (from size chart)	Total	Dress stand size	Amount to add
Bust	88 34⅝"	10 4"	98 38⅝"		
Waist	68 26⅝"	1 (close fit) ⅜" 4 (dresses) 1⅝"	69 27" 72 28⅛"		
Hips	94 37"	5 2"	99 39"		
Nape to back waist	41 16⅛"	none	41 16⅛"		

Tolerance, ease and designer ease

The human body expresses itself in movement: walking, bending, reaching and climbing. For every action made within the garment being worn an allowance (known as 'tolerance') must be incorporated in patterns to avoid the garment creasing and splitting with the strain. Research has determined how much tolerance is needed in woven garments and where it should be added when making patterns. It applies mainly to horizontal movements. Tolerance, therefore, refers to the amount of fabric added to a garment in addition to the exact measurement of the body, to allow for normal body movement.

'Ease' is also an additional amount included in the pattern and fabric. It occurs naturally in the modelling process and some ease is already incorporated into pattern-making blocks. It is needed mainly where a seam consists of quite different shapes, such as the

convex curve of the sleevehead joining the concave shape of the armhole. It does not have to be added on in the same way as tolerance. Other natural 'ease' areas include the bend of the elbow and the bust cup area of a panel seam. The modelling exercises to follow include instructions for placing notches to mark areas to be eased.

'Designer ease' refers to extra amounts of fabric necessary to achieve the garment design, such as lengthening and widening the bodice in a blouson-style dress or incorporating pleats and gathers to achieve a certain silhouette. This is in addition to normal ease and body tolerance.

Tolerance areas for normal body movement

Additional design ease

Whether creating garment designs for standard sizes or for individuals, it is essential to know the measurements of the stand being used or of the individual so that the correct amount of tolerance can be added during the modelling or flat patternmaking.

Without the tolerance, the garment will be skin-tight and split in wear. The tolerances in the charts on pages 12-13 give a close but comfortable fit over under-garments. Extra tolerance should be added to all sizes for a looser fit and some or all tolerances removed for foundationwear (see page 32).

For everyday body movement - excluding sports and other active leisure pursuits - the extra fabric is needed horizontally, as shown in the diagram below. Some of the amounts are very small - from 0.6cm (¼") on the across chest measurement to 10cm (4") on the bust measurement. Measure the stand or the block pattern in use and compare with the body measurement in the size chart. Photocopy the size charts on pages 12 and 13 and keep by the work table as a constant reference to the main body measurements, increments per size and the correct amount of body tolerance to include.

Most movement tolerance is needed horizontally

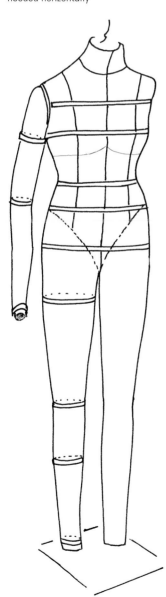

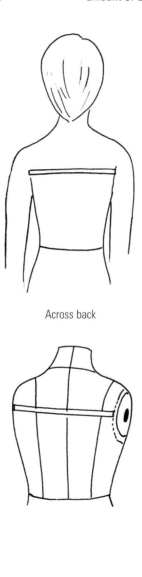

Across back

2. Padding the stand

Some dress stands have body tolerance included, usually by arrangement between garment manufacturers and stand manufacturers. This enables designers to model the fabric to closely fit the stand knowing that sufficient room is already included for body movement and they do not have to pad up the stand or use other methods of incorporating the tolerance. Most stands, however, are constructed to standard body size at bust, waist, hip, nape to back waist and hip length and continue un-shaped for about 20 cm (8") below the hipline, ending in a straight horizontal line, at what would be mid-thigh position on the body or on a stand with legs.

It is sometimes necessary to increase the size of the stand to create larger sizes or to make slight adjustments to width or length in specific areas. It is not possible to make a solid stand smaller, but it can be re-taped to create a higher or lower waistline or re-shaped with padding for raised shoulders or raised hipline. Padding the stand all round will increase the overall girth but care must be taken to keep neck and shoulders in proportion.

Use sheet wadding for padding, which is available in several thicknesses from large fabric and haberdashery stores. Pin the first layer with 'lills' (very short pins). Several layers can be applied and will adhere to each other. Cover the last layer with stretchy fabric such as stretch calico or pieces cut from old pairs of tights.

Adjustable stands have gaps where they expand and these open areas can be taped over with masking tape and a cover made by modelling calico to the shape of the stand seamlines to provide a surface for pinning.

(a) Use masking tape to cover the gaps when enlarging an adjustable stand.

(b) Cover modelled to the stand shape. Pin together at centre back for easy removal.

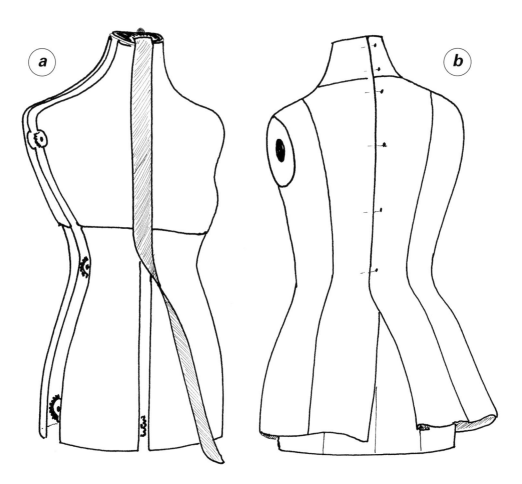

Although the stand can be padded up to increase its size horizontally, the main purpose of padding the stand in this book is to show how to change its shape for different kinds of garment. In the nightwear section, it is useful to raise the shoulders and attach a padded arm for creating shirt-type sleeves for pyjama tops and robes, or to thicken the torso or legs for pyjama trousers. These examples are dealt with as they occur in the text. In close-fitting garments such as bras and 'bodies' the stand is usually too large and the solution for this is demonstrated on pages 30-31.

(a) A bra fastened to the stand indicates where loose areas may need to be padded up with thin strips of wadding pulled from the sheet wadding, shown in more detail in (c).
(b) Hip size increased with sheet wadding with fine muslin or jersey stretched over the wadding.
(c) Upper section of bust lightly padded with fine strips of sheet wadding and the lower bust given a positive shape with a purchased half-cup.
(d) Padded half and full cups are useful for enlarging the bust.

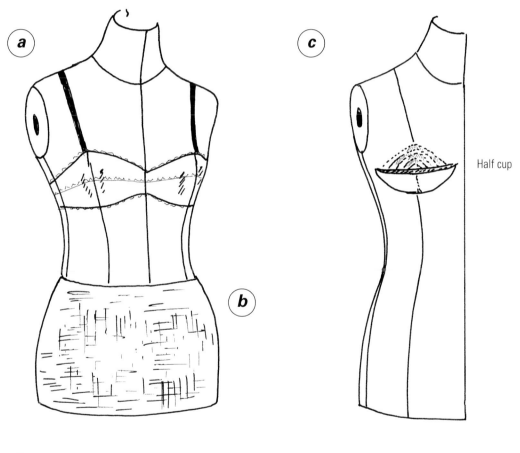

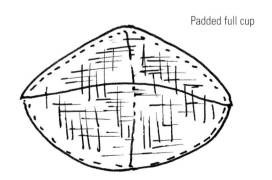

Half cup

Padded full cup

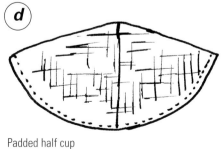

Padded half cup

3. Taping the stand

It is essential to be able to define the main seamlines of the stand for reference during modelling, when they are hidden beneath the modelling fabric. With experience the fingers can follow the seams, but beginners find it helpful to outline them with modelling stay tape, which can be left on permanently as a guide to the main vertical and horizontal body 'lines'. Use 'Lills' (short pins 7mm long) which sink in diagonally and keep narrow tape in place.

Tape all the horizontal seams first. The girth (all round) positions such as bust, hip and high hip are not usually marked on the stand and will need to be measured, taking care to keep each level horizontal to the floor. The shoulder panel lines of the torso stand can be taped from the lower edge of the stand upwards and taken over the shoulder, avoiding a break. The stand with legs can also have the crotch level, thigh, knee, calf and ankle taped and the centre front and back

seam can be taped with one long piece of tape from the base of the front neck, through the legs, up the centre-back seam to the nape, known as the 'through trunk length'. It is also useful to tape the centre-front and centre-back 'crease lines' of the right leg for aligning the fabric straight grain. See suggested order of taping the stand on this page.

The armhole: size 12 armhole depth = 14-15cm (5½-6"); armhole width = 11cm (4⅜").

To tape the armhole, measure and cut a piece of tape 42.6cm (16¾") plus 1cm (⅜") for overlapping. This is the minimum for a size 12 armhole and is divided into approximately 20cm (8") at the back and 22.8cm (9") at the front. Form into a circle and pin to the shoulder point 11.9cm (4¾") from the stand side neckpoint. Pin to sides of stand armhole but take the tape lower than the arm circle marked on the stand to form a flatter curve at the front.

SUGGESTED ORDER OF TAPING THE STAND

HORIZONTAL SEAMLINES	VERTICAL SEAMLINES (Size 12)
Base of neck	Centre-back/ centre-front
Shoulder	Shoulder panel lines to lower edge of torso stand or through to ankle
Across back	About 10.5cm (4⅛") below nape
Chestline	Side seam from underarm
Bust level	Inner leg seam
Waist level	Armhole
High hip (10cm (4") below waist)	Crotch level
Hip (20cm (8") below waist)	
Thigh, knee, calf and ankle	

On the padded arm (page 90) tape the bicep, elbow, mid forearm, wrist, outer and inner sleeve seam and the armhole.

BACK   SIDE   FRONT

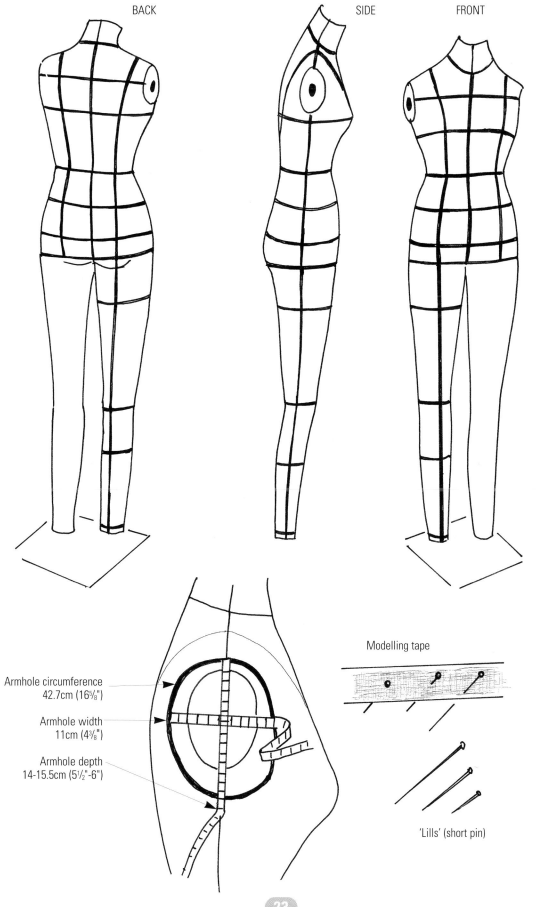

Armhole circumference
42.7cm (16⅝")

Armhole width
11cm (4⅜")

Armhole depth
14-15.5cm (5½"-6")

Modelling tape

'Lills' (short pin)

4. Taping design lines

Narrow tape is used to define the main design lines of a garment. This taping is temporary and changes from style to style. The diagrams show how a sketch is interpreted and its main design lines taped on the stand. When draping fabric without a pre-conceived sketch, design-line taping can be omitted and the fabric modelled directly onto the dress stand 'by eye', manipulating the fabric yet allowing its characteristics to determine the final silhouette and seam positions to achieve perfect harmony between the fabric and the design. Use dressmaker pins or glass headed pins if these will not snag the fabric. They are easy to insert and remove, and stronger than dressmaker pins. The taped seamlines of the stand have been omitted in diagram (b) below to avoid confusion with the design lines. Most stands are light in colour and traditionally black tape is used to define all lines because it shows through the modelling toile but it seems sensible to use different colours where appropriate. With experience only design lines, if any, will need to be taped .

(a) Symmetric designs are modelled on the right-hand side of the stand only, creating a half pattern which is cut from double fabric, producing an identical 'mirror image' for the other half of the body. Buttonstands and their facings overlap the centre of the stand and waistbands and belts are usually modelled all the way round.

(b) Asymmetric designs require both right and left sides of the garment to be modelled and will produce pattern pieces which are not identical.

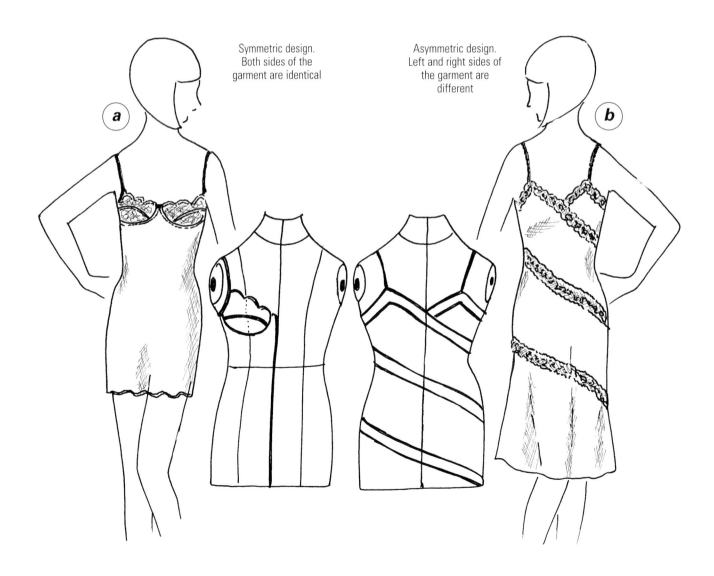

Symmetric design.
Both sides of the garment are identical

Asymmetric design.
Left and right sides of the garment are different

5. Understanding fabric grain

The term 'straight grain' indicates yarn (thread) direction in woven fabrics; the warp means lengthwise, along the length of the fabric and the weft is crosswise, across the width of the fabric. Both are straight grain directions but have different characteristics. The warp thread is tauter and stronger and has very little stretch. For this reason, in most garments, the warp grain runs vertically through garments from shoulder to hem and is the straight grain referred to in pattern instructions. The crosswise grain has more give and is usually placed horizontally across the body. 'Bias' is not a grain but a direction and refers to cuts in other directions to the straight grains. 'True bias' or 'true cross' refer to a direction at an angle exactly 45 degrees from the straight grain.

Knitted fabrics are formed by interlocking loops of yarn and are more flexible in all directions than woven fabrics. The direction of the loops is comparable to the warp and the crosswise comparable to the weft threads of woven fabric.

6. Preparing the fabric for a design

Famous designers are usually photographed working with a roll of fabric trailing from the dress stand or live model onto the floor. Leaving the fabric trailing is appropriate for an elaborate draped design where the designer is making decisions as the design develops and cannot calculate the amount of fabric and cut it to a convenient length. However, the usual practice is to cut pieces of fabric to a workable size, making it quicker and easier to complete the modelling.

7. Controlling the fabric grain vertically and horizontally on the stand

Most garments are cut with the lengthwise grain falling from neck to hem and the horizontal grainline parallel to the floor. On the stand, as on the body, the horizontal grain must be level at bust, waist and hip levels to ensure accuracy throughout the garment. Some fabrics have pronounced threads which show grain direction. Others are so smooth that the grain cannot be accurately detected but it is important to establish it or the finished garment will not hang correctly. The selvedge is a good guide to the lengthwise grain, but where it is absent, pull out a weft thread to see the crosswise direction and the lengthwise warp threads will be at a right angle to this.

When working on the cross, cut the fabric in strips as shown below.

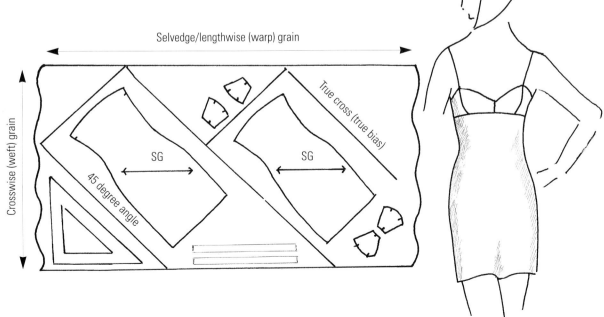

8. Shaping fabric to curves by creating darts

The grapefruit exercise

A simple example of the skill of modelling woven fabric to the shape of the breast can be demonstrated in the following way:

(a) Take half a large grapefruit or other semi-circular object. Measure the dome and mark its centre.
(b) Cut a circle of fabric to this diameter. Mark the exact centre and draw 2 lines through it on the warp and weft threads. Draw a circle 1.5cm (⅝") radius round the centre mark. Darts are pinned and sewn to the edge of this circle.

(c) Pin the centre mark on the fabric to the centre of the object. Smooth the fabric towards the outer edges. Whichever way the fabric is directed there will always be a surplus. Try to eliminate the surplus fabric by forming darts, first one dart, then two, three and four, starting from the outer edge of the fabric and tapering to the outer edge of the bust point circle. Use the grainlines to keep the centres of the darts on a straight fold. Mark the edges of the darts with a coloured pencil. Most darts end 1.5cm (⅝") from the bust point.

(d) Shows all the surplus fabric being formed into one large dart.

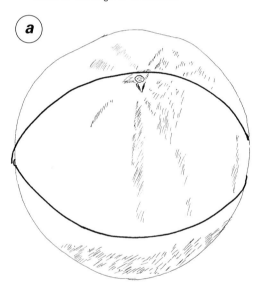

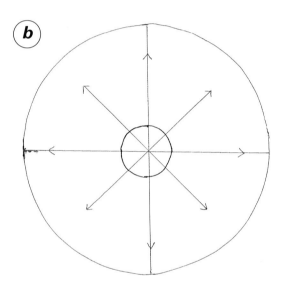

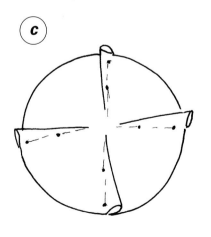

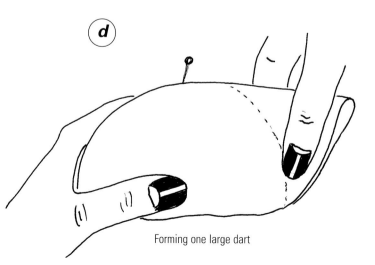

Forming one large dart

Dealing with surplus fabric: modelling the bust shape

(e) Bring surplus fabric equally to either side. Use pins to keep the remainder of the fabric in place.

(f) Pinning from either side on the dart line enables a smoother line to be marked.

(g) Cut through these lines and up to the 'bust point' to create a horizontal seamline.

Now try forming the darts on the true cross of the fabric midway between the marked lines. Which was easier, using the straight grain or the true cross as the dart centre? It takes a little practice to control the true cross or any other bias direction.

It can be seen from the grapefruit exercise that modelling a piece of flat fabric over a curve inevitably leads to surplus fabric which may be formed into darts or cut out to shape seams.

Forming two darts

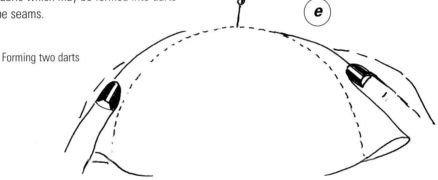

e

Pin each side

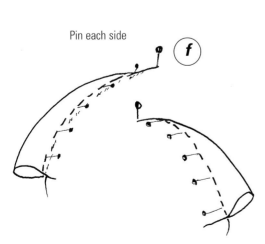

f

Creating a shaped seam
Cut through remaining fabric to 'bust point'

g

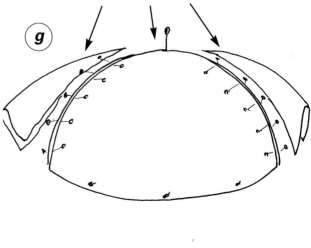

Taping design lines onto the stand provides guidelines for darts and seams.

Practise taping various bra designs onto the stand and modelling small pieces of fabric to the bust shape. Decide which way (if any) the grain goes, usually the vertical straight grain of woven faric is placed along the area of body strain. In a bra the straight grain will be positioned where it gives most support to the breasts. In knitted fabrics regard the vertical lines of loops as the 'straight grain'. Where no grain is apparent, pull the fabric to determine the least flexible direction and regard this area as providing the most support and least likely to sag in wear.

After modelling the shapes required, and cutting surplus fabric down to about 1cm (³⁄₈"), the design lines and notches are marked in pencil or marking pen. Notches are necessary for accurate seam-matching and where one seam needs to be eased to another over the bust curve. The pieces are then removed from the stand and the lines 'trued', which means correcting wobbly lines supposed to be straight and improving the run of curves. It is easier to perfect these on a flat surface. Pin the trued sections onto paper and trace through the marked lines with a tracing wheel.

Mark the paper pattern pieces with the following details:

- design number (if any)
- name of the piece (centre front panel)
- straight grainline
- how many to cut
- centre-front, centre-back, lower cup
- how much seam allowance has been added (if any)
- notches

a

Tape stand

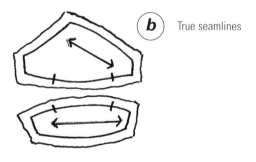

b True seamlines

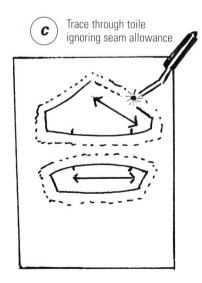

c Trace through toile ignoring seam allowance

Underwear section

Modelling bras: establishing 'cup' size

There is a difference between 'bust' measurement and 'bra' size. When preparing the stand for non-standard size figures, establish the person's bra size, then the 'cup' size and pad the stand to this shape. Although the examples below are shown in both metric and imperial measurements, the conversion from one to the other is still not exact. Work with the figues you are accustomed to using.

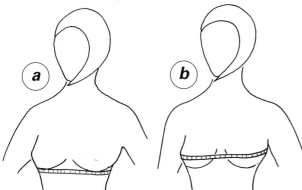

How to establish bra size

(a) Measure the rib cage (all round under the bust) and add 12.5 cm (5").

Example: Rib cage: 84cm (33") plus 12.5cm (5") = 96.5cm (38").

How to establish cup size

(b) Measure the bust at its fullest part. The difference between this and the bra size will determine the cup size.

Example: Fullest measurement: 96.5 cm (38") minus bra size 91cm (36"). The difference is 2" (5cm) = cup size C.

The chart below covers from 1" to 7" (2.5cm to 18cm) difference between the bust measurement and the bra size and covers cup sizes A to FF/G.

(a) Measuring the rib cage girth

(b) Measuring over the fullest part of the bust girth

Difference between bust measurement and bra size

centimetres	inches	cup size
2.5cm	(1") less	cup size is AA
Same	same	cup size is A
2.5cm	(1") more	cup size is B
5.0cm	(2") more	cup size is C
7.5cm	(3") more	cup size is D
10.0 cm	(4") more	cup size is DD
12.5cm	(5") more	cup size is E
15.0cm	(6") more	cup size is F
17.5cm	(7") more	cup size is FF/G

Adjustments to dress stands for skin-tight garments

A lingerie or swimwear stand which closely resembles the body contours enables the modeller to create a toile and copy it onto paper with no further alteration. However, if a dress stand designed for daywear is used, close-fitting garments will be too large and further tightening of the toile is necessary before a final pattern can be obtained. Two methods are in common use. The first is to mark 'tightening darts' on the stand. The second method is to draw the extra darts onto the paper pattern developed from the toile. The first method is quicker and illustrated opposite. If the stand is not your own and it not possible to mark it, *model a close-fitting, removable cover in thin fabric, and mark the main seamlines plus the extra darts on it as illustrated opposite. Leave the centre-back open and pin the cover to the stand only when designing underwear or close-fitting special occasion wear.

* *A lightweight, removable, tubular jersey fabric pulled over the stand can be marked in the same way and is quicker to make than the modelled version.*

In addition to marking the main vertical and horizontal positions on the stand, tape the armhole, rib cage and bust separation and move the side seams forward by 3cm (almost 1¼").

Measuring the bust separation between bust points

Tightening the bust circle after modelling the toile

It is convenient to do this by the flat pattern cutting method. When a dart is folded out or overlapped to tighten one area the same amount must be released into another dart or design line to keep the pattern flat. In a one-dart bra the final dart would be increased by all of these small but significant tightening darts at the point where they encounter the outer bust circle, not the amount where they began on the neckline, armhole or centre-front.

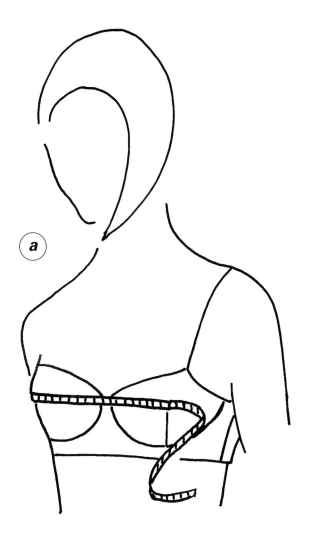

a

The extra darts are marked onto the modelled bra sections before removing them from the stand, then folded out to remove surplus tolerance and more closely fit the figure. The shaped bra sections are pinned to pattern paper, grain lines and notches copied and seam-allowance added to create the final pattern pieces.

The adjustments will tighten the upper garment edge by 2.5cm (1") and the area immediately under the bust by 1cm (⅜"). Bra designs differ considerably but try to keep to the positions shown for making adjustments, which take the surplus fabric from the natural hollows of the body. The same effect is not achieved by taking one large dart, which would distort the garment shape.

To complete the pattern, add 1cm seam allowances and grainlines.

Draw a circle with an 8cm (3¼") radius around the bust point, then draw on the following darts, all radiating from the bust point.

  1cm (⅜") from mid-front armhole to bust point.
  1cm (⅜") from centre-front bustline to bust point.
  1cm (⅜") from mid-way centre front neck point to side neck point.
Mark 0.5cm (-¼") either side of seamline on lower bust circle. Connect upwards to bust point and downwards to normal position at waist.
Mark 0.5cm (-¼") on one side only of stand seamline on upper bust circle. Connect to bust point.

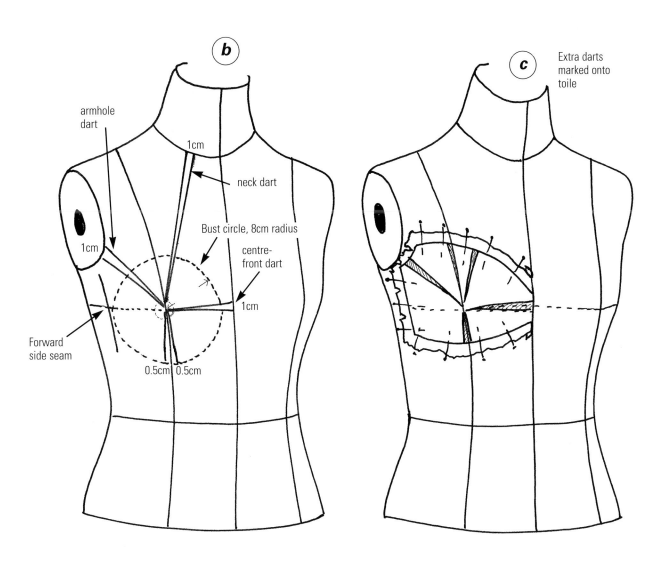

b

armhole dart

1cm

neck dart

Bust circle, 8cm radius

centre-front dart

1cm

1cm

Forward side seam

0.5cm 0.5cm

c Extra darts marked onto toile

Modelling bras with non-stretch fabrics: the darted bra

The techniques used for the control of surplus fabric when modelling the bra in woven or other non-stretch fabrics is not limited to underwear; the same techniques can be used for creating close-fitting bodices in sun dresses, party and eveningwear. The experience is useful because attention has to be paid to the grain direction and bias of the fabric to create a bra which has a beautiful shape and fits properly. The first bra exercises will include shaping the bra with darts, followed by vertical, horizontal, diagonal and curved seams to give a variety of modelling experiences.

Bra with single under-bust dart: pattern

The single-darted bra is less common than the bra with shaped seams. It is included to give experience in controlling all surplus fabric in the bust circle from one position.

Tape the design lines onto the stand

(a) Cut a square of bias fabric 24cm x 24cm (9½" x 9½").

(b) Pin with the straight grain from centre front towards the shoulder strap position, (c) Smooth and pin along the armhole and lower centre front as shown.

(d) Pin the lower side section. The remaining surplus fabric falls below the bust point.

(e) Pin the dart from outer circle to bust point. Trim to 1.5cm (⅝") and mark dart, outer edges and notches.

(f) Under-bra midriff section. Following the taped design lines, pin a small piece of straight grain fabric from centre-front to side seam. Trim and cut off surplus and mark outer lines and notches.

(g) Back section. Pin a back bra fastener to the stand. Pin straight grain of fabric from front side seam as far as the fastener. Trim, remove surplus fabric and mark outer lines and notches. Measure the length of the shoulder seam.

(h) Mark the extra tightening darts onto the toile, remove from stand, true the lines and trace onto paper. Fold out or cut and overlap the tightening darts. The design dart will widen by the amounts closed elsewhere. Final pattern.

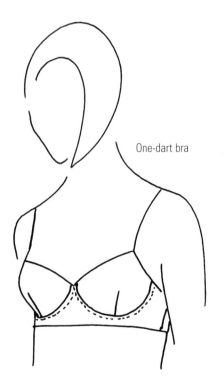

One-dart bra

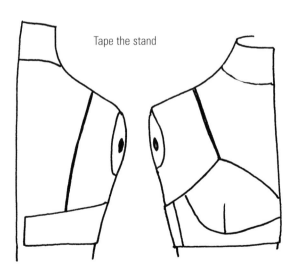

Tape the stand

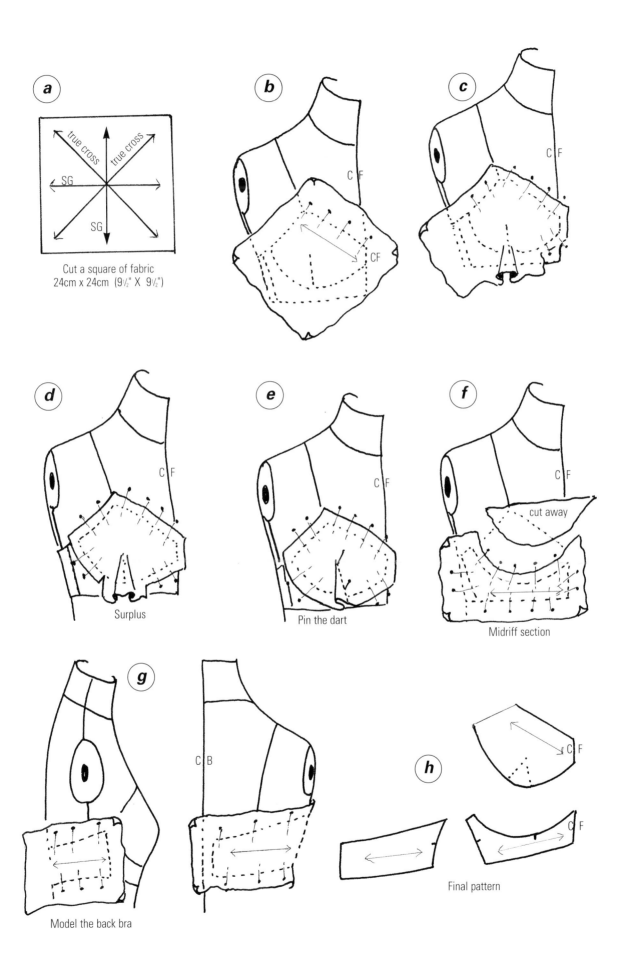

a Cut a square of fabric
24cm x 24cm (9½" X 9½")

true cross   true cross
SG
SG

b CF

c CF

d CF
Surplus

e CF
Pin the dart

f CF
cut away
Midriff section

g Model the back bra
CB

h CF
CF
Final pattern

Bras with cup seams

Instructions for trueing up and extra tightening are not repeated for individual exercises. When modelling in woven fabrics always refer back to pages 30 - 31.

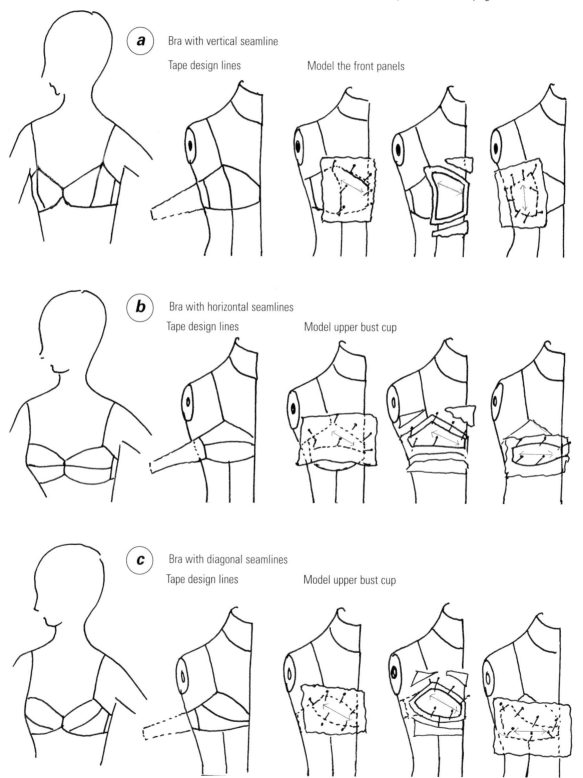

a Bra with vertical seamline

Tape design lines

Model the front panels

b Bra with horizontal seamlines

Tape design lines

Model upper bust cup

c Bra with diagonal seamlines

Tape design lines

Model upper bust cup

Complete front cup, model back bra section, mark and notch seams

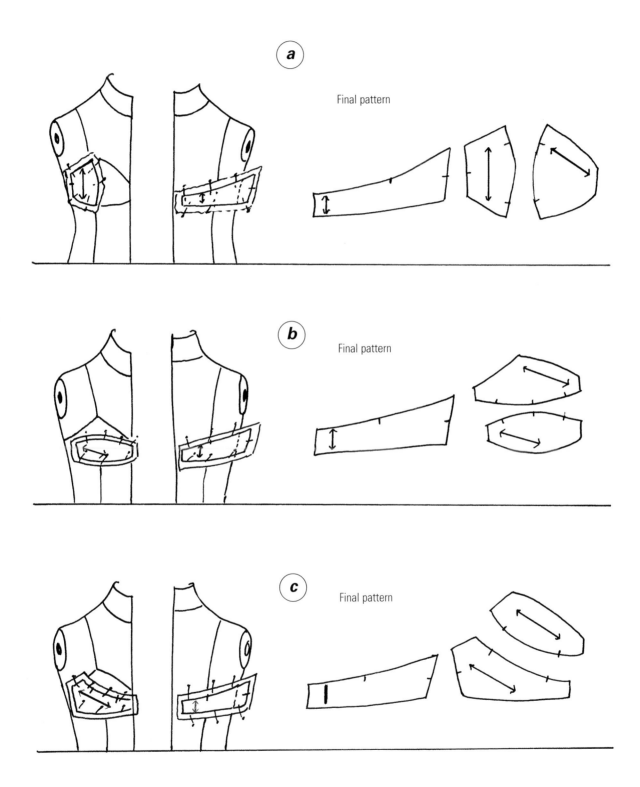

a

Final pattern

b

Final pattern

c

Final pattern

Lace bras

Extra tightening of the bra is only needed if a dress, rather than a lingerie stand is being used. If a lingerie stand is available, the design can be modelled with no alterations except in the case of making to individual measurements rather than to a standard size.

Non-stretch lace may be used instead of a woven fabric. Lace has no grain and the net areas between the motifs allow great flexibilty when modelling. In seamed designs the lace can be eased to fit the bust circle with no difficulty.

Although lace is more flexible than woven fabric, it should not be stretched to fit but smoothed in the same way as modelling with woven fabrics.

When lace motifs have very pronounced edges, position them away from the seams to avoid ridges showing through outer garments. Consider the fabric

DESIGN NOTE

When extra tightening of the bra is needed after modelling the bra toile, use plain fabric to model the design lines, complete the bra pattern then cut out in lace. When lace is modelled directly onto a lingerie or swimwear stand no further alteration is required.

before deciding on a particular bra style and position the lace motifs where they will be most effective.

The edges of cut lace need reinforcing to prevent stretching to retain the close fit and are usually backed with ribbon or tape. It is also quite effective to turn the raw edges of lace over onto the right side and cover them with satin ribbon. Lace edgings can be used and are reinforced with narrow tape to firm the seam.

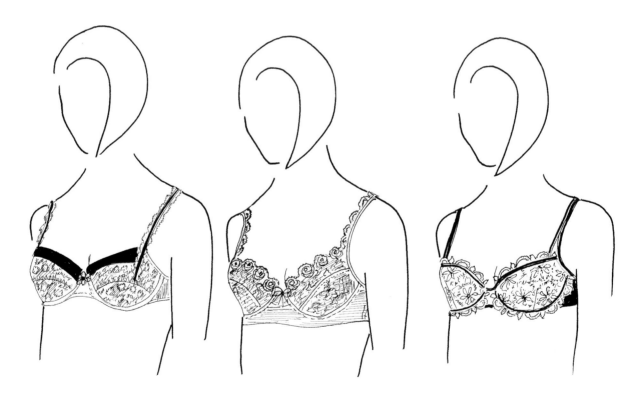

Bra designs using lace

Long line bras

Long line bras extend below the bust circle to cover the ribs and may extend to waist length. Lightweight bones are usually inserted in the panel and side seams although less so when using stretch fabrics. The skin-tight fit gives a smooth line under close-fitting garments and disguises a pronounced rib cage or spare tyre. Extra bands of elastane fabric may be used diagonally to give firmer control as seen in the diagram below. The upper edges between the straps are frequently controlled by backing with narrow ribbon to prevent them stretching and the under bust design line may be wired or reinforced with tape which crosses over at the cleavage to avoid a weak point.

Taken lower than the waist the long-line bra becomes a corselette, a favourite lingerie item in bridalwear. In addition to keeping up stockings the suspenders prevent the corselette from riding up (see page 44).

Model the bust cup as in previous exercises. For the midriff sections cut fabric into straight grain vertical strips and model each panel parallel to the centre-back or front. Remove from the stand, true the lines and trace final pattern onto paper.

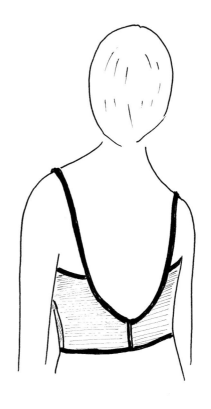

Strapless bras

Strapless bras are needed when the outer garment has no built-in support such as shoulder seams or straps to support the weight of the garment and the bust. Many evening, bridal and sun-dresses include a built-in boned layer, making a separate bra unnecessary.

Strapless bras are modelled in the same way as in the previous exercises but require sufficient built in support to keep them in place. Lightweight but firm boning is usually added to the panel lines and side seams to prevent the garment riding up the body.

Underwiring can be used where the lower half of the bust circle is defined, both in strapless and long-line bras or the seam can be made firm by double stitching or ribbon.

Detachable straps are usually provided so that the bra can also be supported by the shoulders under suitable dresses. The straps can be attached to go over the shoulders, therefore supporting both the back and the front of the garment or round the neck only to wear under 'halter neckline' garments. Halter neckline straps are not connected to the back of the bra, so the fit must be very close to remain in position on the body.

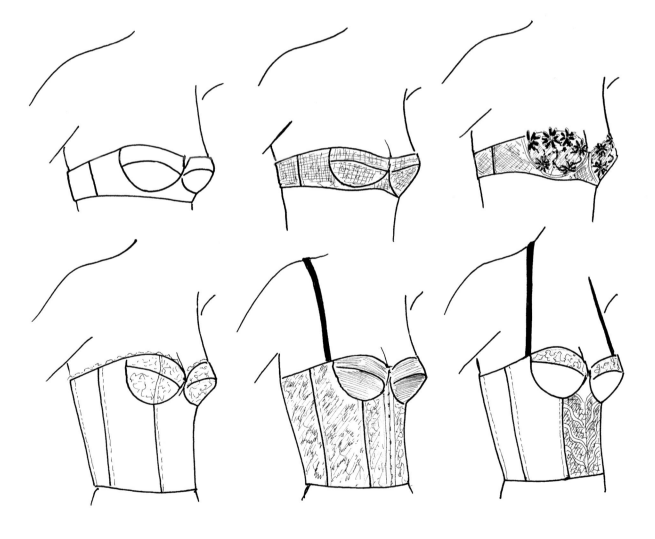

'Bodies' and support pants

Stretch fabrics have made this garment easier to construct than its predecessor, which was made from panels of woven fabric and boning. The modern 'body' is an attractive garment which fits like a second skin. Bodies can also incorporate suspenders for when stockings rather than tights may be worn. The fit should be quite tight to provide support and ensure a smooth line below outer garments. Some designs incorporate a vest and include necklines and sleeves. Instead of a defined bra section as part of the design, a pair of built-in bra support cups can be joined to the side seams, as in the eveningwear body on page 82.

It is difficult to model on only half of the stand when working with stretch fabrics. Cut the fabric wide enough to model across the whole front or back stand. For symmetric designs, only the right-hand side of the bra need be modelled. When constructing the final paper pattern only the right-hand half of the bra will be traced through to ensure a perfect mirror image.

Where bra sections are well defined they are modelled in the same way as separate bras and notches marked for joining to the main part of the garment. See bra instructions on pages 32-39. Crotch gussets may be an extension of the main garment or cut separately. For extended gussets, cut the fabric for the back section longer than the front to go between the legs to the front gusset opening and allow extra fabric for an adjustable fastening. See pages 42-43 for modelling the lower half of the body illustrated.

When working with a stand with two legs, the gusset area is difficult to model because the gap between the legs is so narrow. The minimum crotch width of 7cm (2¾") where there is no centre seam, or 3.5cm (1⅜") from centre-front to groin can be checked when trueing up the lines to make a paper pattern for size 12. The crotch width may be a little narrower for sizes 8 - 10 and widened by up to 0.5 cm (¼") per size from

DESIGN NOTE

A 'body' is a close-fitting garment which incorporates bra and brief, an 'all-in-one' foundation garment which provides a smooth, lightweight layer to protect and support the body. There is usually a defined bra section, the area from rib-cage to crotch is cut with centre back and side seams and the lower opening is constructed towards the front of the extended crotch gusset. The garment must be able to stretch and recover sufficiently to pull over the hips and cling to the midriff. A toile should be made for new designs to determine the exact amount of stretch and recovery in the fabric, particularly if the type of stretch fabric being modelled has not been used previously.

size 14 upwards. Another check measure is the 'through trunk length' measured from nape of neck down through back-waist, beween the legs, up to front-waist and to front-neck base. Remember to deduct the amount from neck to upper edge of 'body' at front and back.

A separate gusset pattern has been provided with the blocks on pages 92-93. The pattern may be used to cut the gusset separately or it may be joined onto the back body to avoid a seam. It will still be necessary to check the measurement between the legs and the crotch width at back and front to ensure correct fit and a smooth seamline. Support pants are modelled in the same way as the lower 'body' but the gusset requires no opening.

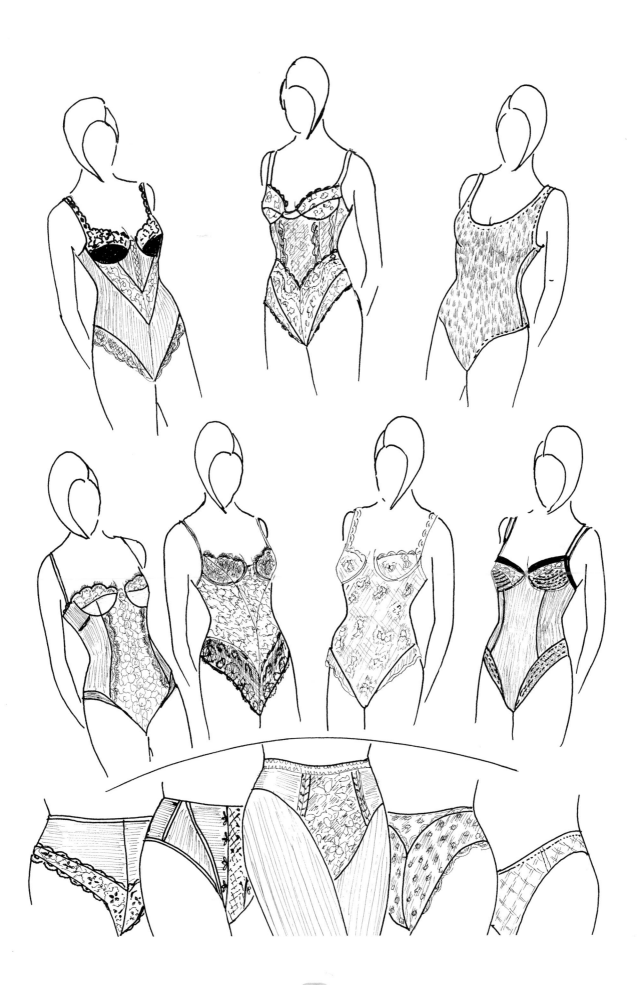

Body in stretch fabric

The body shown opposite has a well-defined bra section. In large sizes, it may be necessary to underline the bra area in a fine but strong matching lining fabric, and to provide extra support by inserting cup-dividers or underwing. Use a strong lingerie elastic for the upper-back edge.

The centre-back seam is optional. If used, however, a separate crotch gusset provides a more comfortable fit between the legs in such a close-fitting garment. In all cases a gusset lining is necessary. The shoulder straps start from the front side seam, encompassing the sides of the bra sections.

NEW TECHNIQUE

Previous instructions have shown the bra sections modelled separately before modelling the torso area. The body design on page 43 shows the torso section extending upwards to the armhole at the sides and to the cleavage at centre front. This provides an opportunity to take one strip of fabric for the entire front. Define the under-bust line and lower section first. Remember to leave seam allowances.

It is only necessary to model the righthand-side bra section. Use the fabric pieces left over from the front torso.

Instructions

Test the stretch and recovery of the fabric before modelling to make sure the garment can be pulled down over the widest part of the hips, otherwise an opening is necessary, as in woven garments.

(a) Tape design lines on front and back stand, including shoulder straps, bust cup seams and the gusset opening between the legs. This is situated towards the front in close-fitting foundationwear for convenient opening, but may be towards the back in looser garments such as cami-knickers.

(b) Cut fabric lengths for front and back sections, plus suffficient to take the back piece between the legs for a continuous crotch gusset. Threadmark the centre of each fabric length for the centre-front and centre-back respectively.

Front

(c) Align the threadmarked centre of the fabric to the centre-front stand seam with surplus fabric above the upper neckline and enough below to reach the crotch opening. Pin at intervals to crotch level.

(d) Smooth fabric from centre-front to side seamlines and pin, snipping in close to the seamline. Cut away surplus fabric.

(e) Continue to pin the threadmarked centre-front to the centre-front stand seamline between the legs as far as the marked gusset opening position, then to each side to complete the front leg shaping, leaving a 1.5cm ($5/8$") seam allowance. Pin and trim under bra seamline, model the bra sections, mark seamlines and notches.

(f) Model the back section, smoothing the fabric out over the buttock area and taking the gusset section through the legs to meet at the front opening position. Mark all seams and notches. Remove the toile from the stand and true the lines. Check the crotch width – 8cm ($3 1/8$"). Trace marked seamlines onto pattern paper and add 1cm ($3/8$") seam allowance to all edges. Cut a separate crotch gusset to be inserted as a lining. See page 93.

(g) Final pattern.

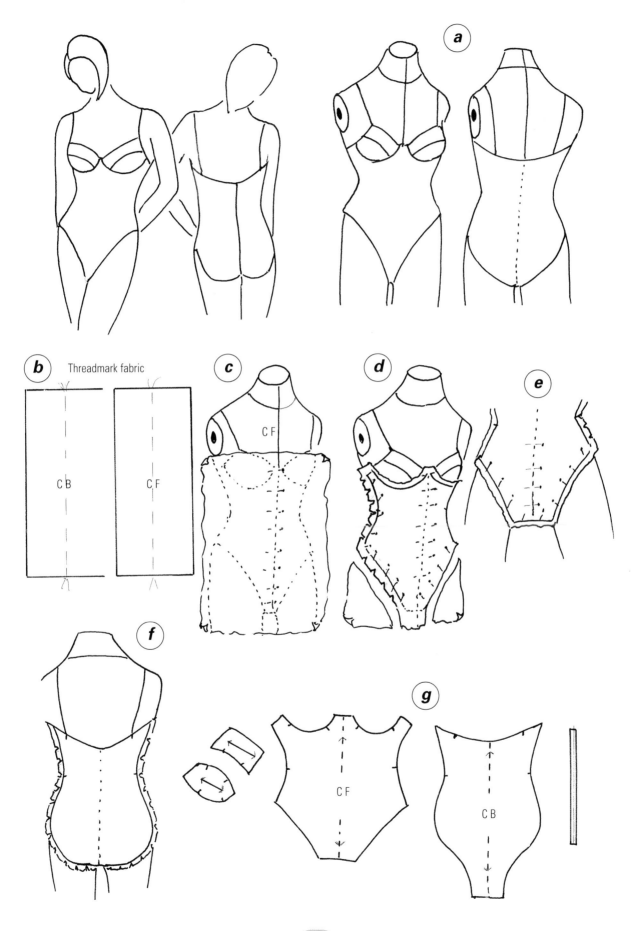

a

b Threadmark fabric

C B

C F

c C F

d

e

f

g

C F

C B

Corselettes, waspies, pantie girdles and suspender belts

Support below the waist

When a separate bra is worn and where some control of the lower body shape is needed the new stretch fabrics have made it possible for designers to create attractive variations of the waist-level corset. Close-fitting girdles can now incorporate strong bands of matching elastomeric fabric to shape, firm and control the body below the waist, yet include bands and edgings of lace. The pantie girdles may be extended to cover the upper thigh for a smooth look under close-fitting skirts, to knee-length or lower for wearing beneath culottes and trousers.

Model girdles and support briefs quite tightly to fit the body exactly. Follow the directions for the lower part of the 'body' on page 43 to model the pantie girdle.

Waspie

This foundation garment reduces the waist size and smooths the midriff and upper stomach. It has no bust cups. Model the waspie tightly. Leave a gap of 5cm (2") at the opening (usually at centre-front). Laces enable the garment to be adjusted throughout its length and close the gap, reducing the body

measurement by one size. Light boning is suggested at the side and panel seams to prevent the upper part sliding down or wrinkling. The instructions for tights (opposite) include the necessary techniques for skin-tight fitting nether garments. For the garments illustrated below, simply tape the stand with the required design lines.

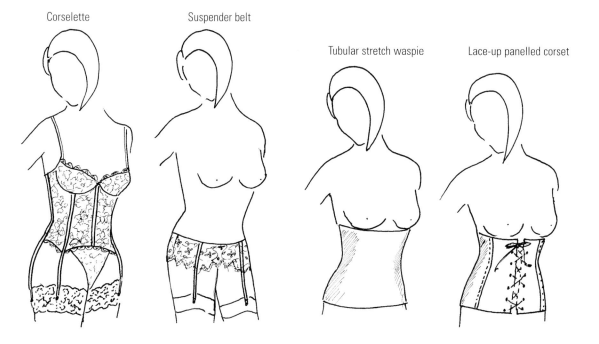

Corselette   Suspender belt   Tubular stretch waspie   Lace-up panelled corset

Modelling tights in superstretch lycra or similar fabric

Cut two lengths of fabric to length required, approximately 102cm (40") long for full-length waist to ankle tights. For the width measurement, measure the top of the back leg at its widest (crotch level) from side seam to inner leg and add 5cm (2").

Use a stand with legs and tape the design lines including the centre-front leg and side seams. For tights with a centre-back and centre-front seam, model on half the stand only. The vertical straight grain or row of knitted loops in jersey should be in line with the centre-front and centre-back of the legs.

(a) Pin fabric to stand following front leg seamline, allowing approximately 2cm (¾") to overlap the side seam at the hip and the remainder to extend beyond the centre-front stand seam. From waist to crotch level, smooth and pin fabric to side and centre front seamline.

(b) Smooth fabric towards inner and outer leg seams and pin from crotch level to ankle. Mark seamlines and notches and trim surplus fabric to 2cm (¾") Unpin side and leg seams and anchor pin away from the seamline while modelling the back tights.

(c) Shows inner leg seam on a one legged stand for clarity.

(d) Model the back tights in the same way, stretching fabric to encompass the seat curve and complete the inner leg seam. Mark, notch and trim surplus fabric.

(e) Completed back leg.

Unpin the side and inner back leg seams, then pin the back and front seams together to check seam runs. Correct if necessary. Remove toile from stand, true up and trace off to make the pattern.

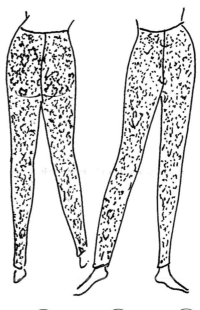

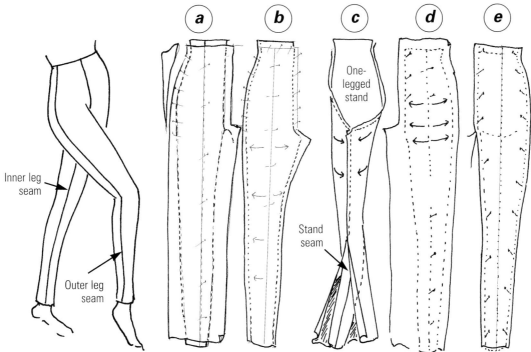

a **b** **c** **d** **e**

One-legged stand

Inner leg seam

Outer leg seam

Stand seam

Briefs, thongs and french knickers

Briefs may be waist high, hipster, bikini or thong. All are 'step in' garments pulled up from feet to waist, which must be wide enough to pull up over the hips. All briefs are a close fit but not necessarily as tight as foundationwear. A casing may be made and elastic inserted or lingerie elastic stitched to the waist and legs. Model in stretch fabric, cotton jersey or cotton and polyamide.

Without centre-back or centre-front seams, either a separate or an extended gusset is needed between the legs. The instructions for briefs on page 47 show a gusset extended from the front and seamed to the back. Diagram (e) also illustrates the two-seam separate gusset.

Model across the whole stand for both front and back brief. Use the gusset pattern on page 93 for the crotch gusset. Crotch width = 8cm (3⅛"). Crotch length = 16cm (6¼"). Add 1cm (⅜") seam allowance, cut out in calico and pin to the stand. Complete the leg shaping. Mark the seams, remove from the stand and complete the pattern, marking centre-back and centre-front 'Place to fold of fabric'. The gusset is cut double.

The thong crotch width is frequently narrower than that suggested for most briefs and can narrow further at the back where there is only a strap to join it to the upper edge.

French knickers are a loose fit all round, have longer legs and are usually cut with centre seams extending between the legs as shown in the tights on page 45, making a separate crotch gusset unnecessary. The crotch depth is lower than in briefs and the back seam length is increased. French knickers require different modelling techniques to any encountered so far (see page 48).

French knickers

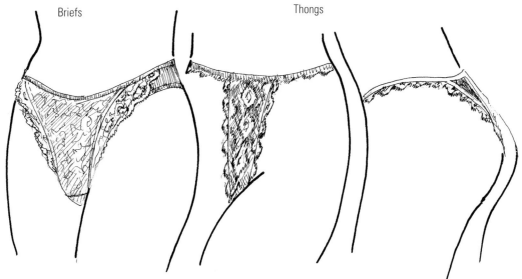

Briefs

Thongs

Briefs

(a) Fabric pinned to centre front stand seam, waistline and front legs and trimmed to 1.5cm ($^5/_8$").

(b) Fabric is cut away leaving remaining fabric hanging for through-leg gusset.

(c) Where the gusset is seamed at the front, the surplus fabric is cut away.

(d) Modelled back view.

(e) Shows shape of briefs with a separate gusset seamed to back and to front brief.

(f) Shows extended front gusset seamed to back brief. A gusset lining would still be cut and a machine line would show at the front but this would not be a seam.

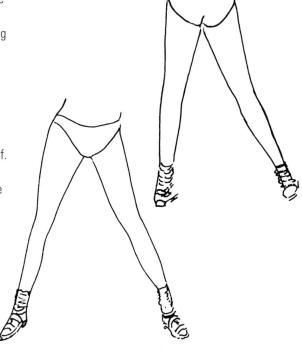

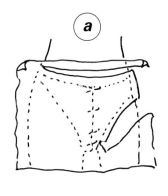

a

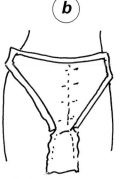

b

No front croch seam

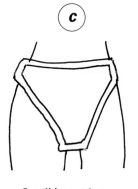

c

Cut off for crotch seam

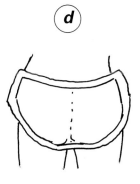

d

Back view

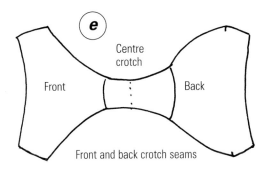

e

Centre crotch

Front

Back

Front and back crotch seams

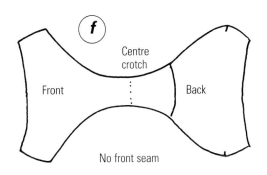

f

Centre crotch

Front

Back

No front seam

NEW TECHNIQUE

Modelling to obtain extra width using gathers and flare

French knickers are fairly loose and call for a different technique from the close-fitting garments discussed previously. The gusset is an extension of the back and front garment sections and joins in the centre, not towards the front as in bodies. It is not possible to tape the looser leg or looser crotch seam on the stand (a) but the required effect can be obtained by judging the width as modelling progresses. The diagrams also show how a circle of elastic can be stretched to the leg width required and the same device used to judge waist fullness (b). Diagram (c) shows the difference between a close and a loose crotch seam and (d) suggests using pre-gathers or a tuck to control the extra fabric width required.

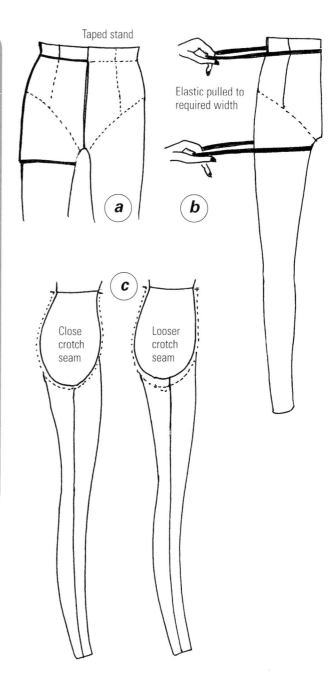

(a) Tape design lines onto the right hand side of the stand: waist, crotch seam from centre-back waist through legs to centre-front waist, side seam. The crotch seam will be modelled lower than the stand, which is body size, to allow for movement. The tape will touch the stand; only the fabric will hang loose.

(b) Cut two squares of fabric 47 cm (18½") Mark centre-front and centre-back 12.5cm (5") in from edge to allow for the crotch shaping. Use gathers or a tuck or pleat to control the fabric width.

(c) Align centre-front to front stand seamline. Pin down to crotch level. Cut off surplus fabric to this level. Anchor pin fabric to stand while the crotch seam is modelled.

(d) Complete the crotch shaping in the same way as the tights on page 45 but much looser, about 2.5cm (1") lower for comfort. Remove anchor pin.

(e) Pin the side seam to the hip level. Allow the fabric to fall free. Model the back in the same way. Remove from stand, true up and trace onto paper.

(f) Final pattern.

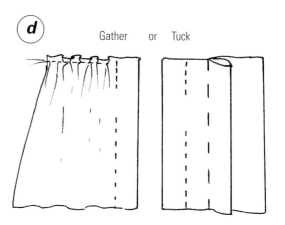

French knickers

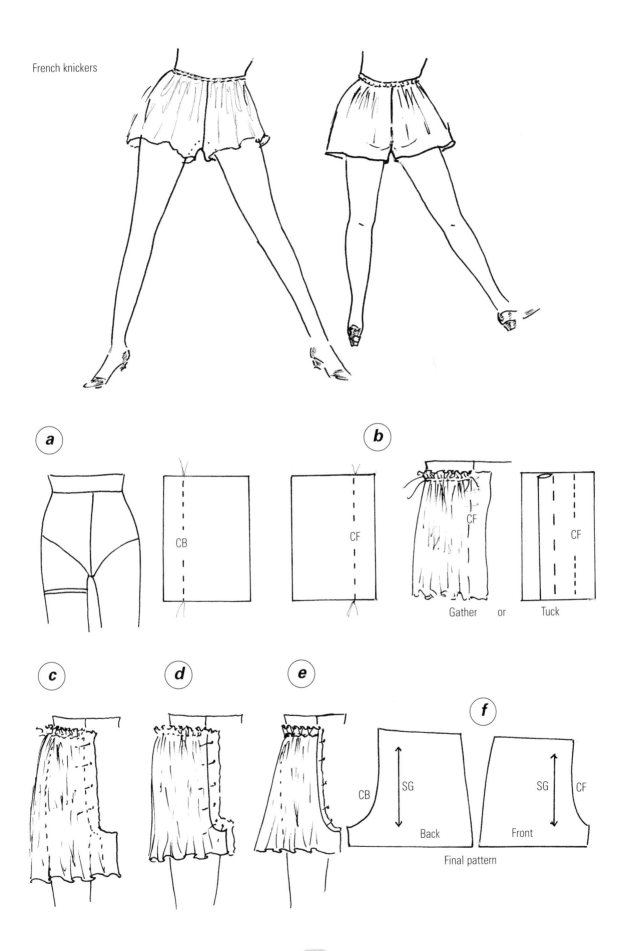

a

CB

CF

b

CF

CF

Gather   or   Tuck

c

d

e

f

CB · SG · Back

SG · CF · Front

Final pattern

Vests, camisoles and slips

Vests may be to rib cage, waist or below hip-length, sleeveless, short or long-sleeved, high or low-necked and made up in any fabric with a little stretch. Once made with scoop neck and shoulder seams they are now designed with various necklines and shoulder straps. Modern fabrics, colours and design have elevated this once practical undergarment whose function was to keep the body warm into an attractive top which can be worn for sports and leisure activities or as partywear. See 'Underwear as eveningwear', pages 82-90.

Model the vests in the same way as bodies but not as close-fitting. They may be worn over a body or bra and support pants, or next to the skin. Those shown on this page have matching briefs. The bust cups may be defined or ignored and any extra support is unnecessary if a body or bra is to be worn beneath.

(a) Below-waist length vest with lace-trimmed, low V-shaped neckline and narrow shoulders with matching lace-trimmed briefs.
(b) Stretch-lace, waist-length vest with minimal bust shaping and matching, panelled brief.
(c) Stretch cotton-jersey crop top in tubular fabric (no seams except at the shoulder) with swim-suit-type back strap. The fabric is pulled onto the stand, the design lines marked and cut all in one piece with no seams. Allow 1cm (³/₈") outer turnings and elasticate the lower edge to prevent it riding up.

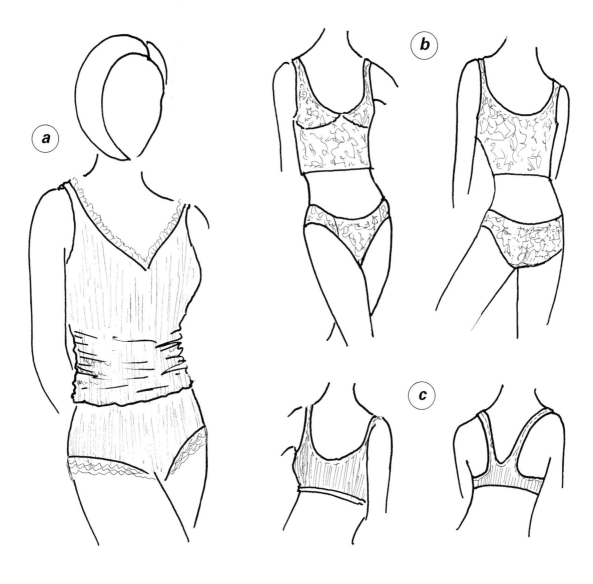

Slips and camisoles

Camisoles cover the top part of the body to just below the waist and are a short version of the slip. When women began to wear trousers the lower half of the slip became unnecessary but the camisole remained. Half-slips suspended from the waistline became popular when skirts and blouses of different colours were worn, such as a white or pastel camisole under a light-coloured blouse with a black half slip beneath a dark-coloured skirt. Wearing a camisole and a half-slip however adds bulk at the waistline and enterprising manufacturers reduced this to one seam at the waist in the two-tone slip - light coloured top and dark skirt (see page 54).

Garments which pull on over the head need to stretch over the shoulders and bust. This can pose a problem when using woven fabrics, which need seams or darts to shape the garment to the body. If cut on the straight grain, an opening is necessary in a full slip unless the fit is to be fairly loose.

By cutting the garment on the bias however, a greater degree of stretch is achieved. Fabrics with some degree of stretch allow slips to be cut on the straight grain without the need for an opening. Camisoles are usually cut on the straight grain and lingerie elastic stitched to the waistline to control surplus fabric. Stretch and non-stretch fabrics can be used in the same garment. For instance, the top of a bra slip in stretch fabric and the skirt in non-stretch, or the whole upper half in stretch and the skirt in non-stretch. Many variations are possible.

The garment should be comfortable both over foundation garments and beneath outer garments and the finish as smooth as possible, particularly under close-fitting tops and dresses.

DESIGN NOTE

Slips and camisoles were first designed to cover foundation garments, to keep them clean and to prevent their pronounced seams and boning from showing through to the outer garment, although this is less so since stretch fabrics have been used in bras, bodies and support briefs. The extra layer between foundationwear and outer garments also protected the skin from contact with fabric, important where fabrics were not washable.

Lace detail abounds in undergarments but lingerie designers are careful to avoid heavy laces whose motifs may show under close-fitting blouses and tops. The main fabric may be woven, knitted or of lace but should be lightweight. Straps may be of ribbon, rouleau or lace. Hems may be narrowly stitched or lace-edged.

Modelling camisoles and slips in woven fabrics requires a different technique to that used for foundation wear, which concentrates on achieving a very close fit.

The following pages will show how to introduce 'designer ease' in the form of a generally looser overall fit, how to add skirt flare and how to deal with woven and stretch fabrics in the same design. Bias-cut fabrics will be modelled across the whole of the stand to maintain the true bias at centre-front and centre-back.

The classic slip on the true bias

The main part of the slip is in two sections (back and front) each cut from single-layer fabric cut on the cross and modelled across the whole of the stand. Unlike straight grain fabric, which can be controlled by pins on the stand centre seam, the flexible nature of bias fabric makes it more difficult to control. Thread-mark the centre and keep it level with the stand centre seams when modelling.

Cut two lengths of fabric for front and back on the true cross (see cutting plan below).
Length = upper edge to hem plus 10cm (4") by hip width plus 10cm (4").

Fold each piece in half lengthwise, lightly finger crease the centre, unfold and threadmark. (If calico is used for the toile a marking pen can be used.)
The remaining triangular pieces will be used for the bust sections.

(a) Tape the whole stand but only model one side (RS) for the bust cup, for which one pattern is made and cut from double fabric.
(b) Position straight grain of a small piece of fabric, approximately 25cm x 25cm (10") from centre front to front shoulder strap position, leaving about 10cm (4") above. Anchor pin bust point and lower edge near centre-front.
(c) Smooth fabric, allowing a little ease from shoulder strap point to side seam at underarm or make a 2cm (¾") tuck (released later) for the easy fit required in a slip. Pin the side seam.
(d) Smooth fabric from centre-front and side seam position towards the bust prominence and below it. The surplus fabric is now all below the bust point.
(e) Form into soft pleats or leave as ease to be gently gathered to fit the lower slip.

Lower slip

(f) Align and pin the marked centre of one piece of bias fabric to centre-front stand seam. Smooth across to side seam at hip level and pin. Leave surplus fabric at side.
(g) Smooth midriff fabric towards side seams. Pin to the under-bust seamline, cutting surplus fabric above the seamline to within 1.5cm (5/8") of seam. Pin remainder of side seam, mark all seams and mark notches for pleats or gathering.
(h) Complete the back slip. Measure over the shoulder for shoulder strap length. Remove toile from stand. True up and trace final pattern onto paper.
(I) Final pattern.

Single layer fabric

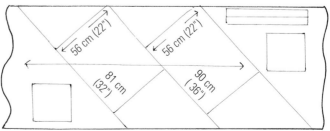

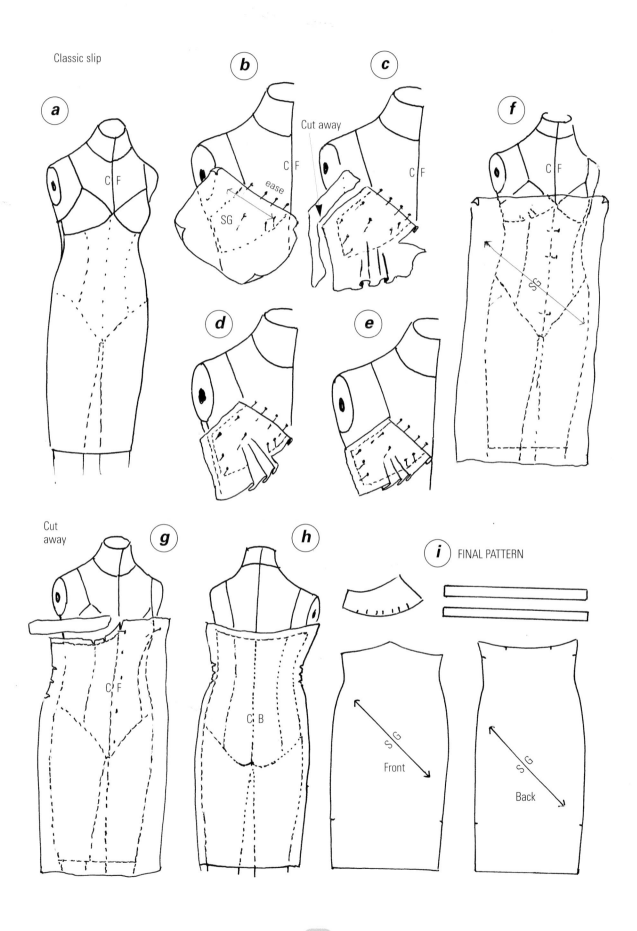

Classic slip

a

b

c

Cut away

ease

SG

f

SG

d

e

Cut away

g

C F

h

C B

i FINAL PATTERN

SG
Front

SG
Back

Lace as applied decoration

The sketches below show various ways of using edging lace and individual lace motifs in slip design. The toiles are modelled first to their full length as if without added decoration. Lace is then positioned on the toile and its outline marked before removing the toile from the stand. There is no need to mark a narrow lace finish.

(a) The hem is decorated with a narrow lace edging which is sewn over the overlocked edge and hangs partly beneath it. For the upper edge, place the lace in position to match either side of centre-front and mark this outline on the toile. It may be sewn onto the finished garment leaving the fabric beneath it intact (appliqué) or the fabric beneath may be cut away (decoupé). 'Shadow appliqué', where a different colour background is visible through the lace, is particularly effective.

(b) Bra-slip with optional halter neck. Model the bra section first, then the lower slip as shown in previous exercises. The lower skirt band is a double-edged lace band. Measure the width of the lace and shorten the toile length by this amount.

c) Two-tone slip. The upper lace is positioned between two well-defined design lines which should be marked on the toile. The top line is the upper garment edge; the lower line depends on the width of the lace. Pin the lace to the shaped bust contours before removing the toile from the stand. Allow sufficient waist width to pull over the head or use a side placket.

d) Lace band added to upper edge and above the hem, then trimed with ribbon, or an insertion lace can be used and the under-fabric trimmed away. The upper band needs to be shaped to follow the design line by mitring at centre front and above the bust points in line with the shoulder straps.

Adding lace edgings and motifs

In woven and knit fabric lingerie garments, lace continues to be the most sought-after decorative finish. It may be added to edges, inserted to form horizontal bands or vertical panels, shaped to replace part of the main fabric as seen in (c) and (d) on page 56 or scattered randomly over the surface as single motifs (see pages 64 and 67). Elaborate lace motifs are manufactured in many sizes to match all-over lace for the lingerie, bridal and eveningwear markets. Lace motifs may also be cut from all-over lace or lace edgings to obtain individual replicas of the main flowers or leaf shapes and applied to the fabric surface.

The positions of lace insertions, panels and motifs are usually determined on the stand while the toile is being developed, particularly where they follow the bust contours. Motifs placed towards the hemline are easier to deal with on a flat surface, such as an ironing board, their approximate positions having already been marked on the stand. Lay a piece of paper or card beneath the fabric to avoid pinning it to the ironing board cover.

The elaborate motif shown in the slip (a) on page 54 would be purchased ready-made and only needs to be stitched to overlap the upper edge, providing a delicate finish on the skin. The edging lace for the hem and remainder of the upper edges, plus the smaller individual motifs at the skirt hem would exactly match the main motif. Many manufacturers now include photographs of a wide range of matching edgings, insertions and motifs in their catalogues and provide a mail order service (see Suppliers list, page 94).

Small lace motifs are frequently used to serve more than one purpose. Besides being a focal point of the garment design, a motif at the centre front seam join of a bra or slip disguises and strengthens a potentially weak construction point. Similarly, the joining of shoulder straps to the garment is less obvious beneath a decorative motif.

Wide shoulder straps of lace, or decorated with lace motifs and backed with soft fabric, are now aesthetically acceptable and comfortable to wear. Wide shoulder straps provide more support than narrow straps, which can cause obvious dips in the centre of womens' shoulders.

A string of motifs can be used very effectively to provide a decorative finish to a seam joining two different types of fabric together or to soften the obvious joins of variously positioned panels and bands in support panties and bodies (see page 41). Placed diagonally, a string of motifs can give an asymmetric impression on an otherwise plain expanse of fabric. The band of lace insertion in the nightdress on page 61 effectively divides the lace bodice from the gathered skirt, whereas the wide lace insertion panels in the tucked nightdress on page 62 provide a delicate contrast to the bands of tucking in the bodice.

DESIGN NOTE

Camisoles provide the same functions as slips but cover only the upper part of the body. Traditionally a fairly loose under-bodice to cover foundationwear and extending to below the waist to tuck into a skirt, they are now made in many types of fabric and designed to be worn as day, evening and nightwear (see the sequinned and metallic fabric camisoles on page 87).

The waist may be left loose or gently elasticated to keep the garment tucked inside skirt or trousers. Extra length for the blouson effect needs to be added just above the waistline. The amount can be judged during the modelling process by tying a piece of elastic round the stand waistline - over the toile - and pulling the bodice fabric upwards to float above it for about 5cm (2") as shown opposite.

Model camisoles in the same way as slips, with or without bust shaping and fairly loose, on the straight grain or the bias and cut off between waist and hip level.

(a) Waist-length button through camisole with upper lace edging.
(b) Below-waist, loose-fitting camisole with centre panel of lace and ribbon bands with the narrow ribbon trim extending to form the shoulder straps.
(c) Wide lace with a scalloped edge is modelled with a seam to provide some bust shaping. Notice how the eye is taken from the ribbon shoulder straps in an unbroken line to the deep V at centre front. The French knickers have matching lace insets.
(d) Blouson camisole with wide straps. The fabric behind the central lace motif is cut away to reveal the skin.
(e) Camisole with lower lace insertion band. The ribbon and narrow edging lace are repeated on the neck edge.

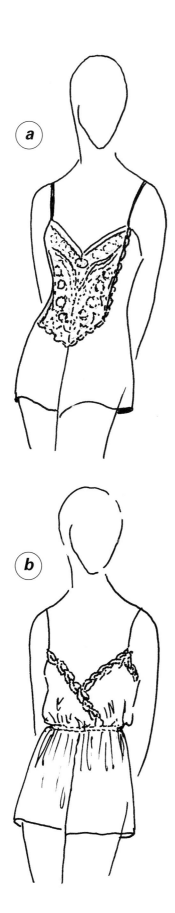

Camiknickers

The crotch length refers only to the distance from front to back waist through the legs. Take a similar measurement from the nape, through back waist, between the legs and up to the front neck base to find the 'through trunk length' (see page 40). Both are close-fitting measurements to which the extra crotch depth can be added by lengthening the centre-back and centre-front seams.

Camiknickers combine the camisole with French knickers but need a crotch gusset with an opening. As with all nether garments, the fit between the legs is a prime consideration and the bent or seated figure would be very uncomfortable and its movement restricted without this extra length. Whereas bodies and briefs require a very close fit, that of knickers and camiknickers is looser, but not as loose as in a pyjama trouser (see page 71). For a loose camiknicker (without waist elastic) add a minimum of 2cm (³/₄") to the 'through trunk' length – for blouson styles add a further 5cm (2") extra above the waist.

Tape the design lines on the stand and follow previous instructions to complete the exercises.

Most camiknickers can be cut without a join at the waistline for blouson styles. A casing can be made for elastic or a lingerie elastic machined-in, soft side outwards because it touches the skin. Where the style is asymetric, as in the wrapover style shown below, the bodice is cut separately and joined to the knickers at the waistline. Notice the increased length of the bodice needed to produce the blouson style.

Straight and flared half slips

Half slips may be stepped into or pulled over the head. In either case the garment must be wide enough to pull over the hips with extra width for bending and sitting. For wear under straight skirts avoid too much extra fabric. Unless the length is very short, walking room must be allowed, usually as a centre-back or side splits. Side seams can be eliminated by having only a centre-back seam.

Extra fullness can be included as gathers. This may be introduced during the modelling or by pinning out a tuck in the fabric (released later) or by gathering (see French knickers on page 48-49).

Both half slips and culotte slips may have briefs or other types of pantie built in to create a single garment which eliminates an extra band of elastic round the waist.

a) Toile for straight half-slip with side seams. Cut two pieces of fabric - length = waist to hem plus 3cm (1¼") by one quarter hip size plus 5cm. Mark the vertical straight grain and a horizontal line to mark the hip level onto the right hand side of the stand.

Fold under the outer (centre-front) edge and align to the stand centre-front. Smooth across to hip level, allowing a good centimetre tuck for extra ease throughout the garment (gives 4cm [1½"] ease all round). Shape the side seam above the hip or leave it straight.

Model the back in the same way, leaving lower seam open. Mark the side seams, waistline and hem level. Remove from stand, true the lines and trace through to make the paper pattern. The waist may include 1.5cm (⅝") for a casing or 0.7cm (a good ¼") turned to the wrong side and lingerie elastic attached.

(b) Culotte slip. A slip with legs - ideal under trousers - can be modelled like French knickers but with smooth, straight legs. A brief can also be incorporated into the waist elastic. Model the briefs first, then the culotte over the top.

(c) Half-slip with curved split, easy to overlock.

(d) Straight half-slip with built-in briefs. Briefer panties may be used.

a Straight half-slip with side split

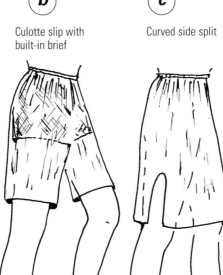

b Culotte slip with built-in brief

c Curved side split

d Straight half-slip with built-in briefs

Flared half-slip on yoke

Half-slips may be flared from the waist or a yoke-line. Flare is introduced by cutting along the upper edge, snipping almost to the marked seamline and allowing the fabric to fall towards the centre. The amount of flare introduced depends on the number of times this process is repeated and by how much the fabric is allowed to fall. This in turn depends on the fabric width, which must be sufficient to complete a whole front or back, unless a centre seam is required.

(a) Tape yoke-line on stand. If a smooth yoke is required, a side or centre-back opening is necessary. Construct the yoke by flat pattern cutting as shown in (e).

(b) Work on half the stand. Align straight grain of fabric to centre-front stand seamline and pin a few centmetres along the yoke-line. Cut away surplus fabric to 1.5cm ($^5/_8$") and snip to seamline. Allow fabric to fall towards centre-front to produce flare

(c) Repeat the process as far as the side seam allowing a little ease along the yoke-line.

d) Allow fabric at the side seam to hang free and cut on a diagonal to produce side flare. Repeat the process for the back. Mark seamlines and notches and remove from stand. True up and trace pattern onto paper.

(e) Measure the front and back yoke lines on the pattern separately and the yoke depth on the stand. Draw two rectangles to these measurements. Add a 2cm ($^3/_4$") casing along the top edge. The diagrams illustrate how a shaped yoke would fit into the rectangle.

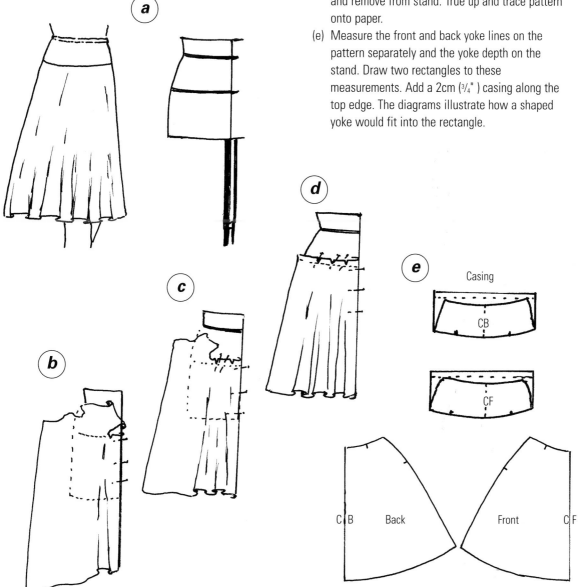

Nightwear section

The human body 'turns over' at least forty times during one night's sleep. Legs and arms stretch, all without conscious thought or consideration for the garment being worn. Stretch fabrics can take the strain of involuntary movement and many fabrics now include some stretch yarn, but traditional woven fabrics without the stretch factor require extra tolerance built into the garment. The examples which follow demonstrate various techniques for achieving fullness on the dress stand, including flares, tucks, and gathers.

Lower underarms and wider sleeves will be introduced in this section, including 'grown-on sleeves' in the form of raglan and kimono.

A pair of padded arms, pinned to the dress stand makes the task of modelling of such garments easier and instructions can be found on page 90-91 for adjusting an existing sleeve pattern to make a pattern for a padded arm. Cut from double fabric, seam like a tight sleeve and stuff to represent a pair of arms.

b
Sleeveless negligee with frilled cape collar (see page 66)

c
Long flared nightdress with layered skirt (see page 64)

a
Tiered top in voile with matching French knickers (see page 63)

Long nightdress with deep plunge stretch-lace top and gently gathered skirt

Two strips of wide, double-edged stretch-lace form the bodice and are linked to the gently gathered skirt by a narrower, double-edged stretch insertion lace. Back and front are the same design, linked low under the arm by an insertion of the main fabric. If the final fabric is modelled directly, fold the skirt fabric double and treat as a single layer (see new technique on page 66).

Attach padded arms to stand (a). Tape design lines onto stand, including the high shaped waistline and a parallel line above it the width of lace used. Cut two lengths of fabric for skirt from highest point to ankle. Fold each through centre, tack together and treat as one layer. Machine gather the top edge. Cut two lengths of the wide lace to go over the shoulders from front to back without a seam.

Align fold of double fabric to centre front stand seamline. Anchor-pin the gathered top edge across to the side seam. On the lower of the two taped lines, pin into rough gathers and pin onto the taped line. Cut away surplus fabric above the high waist (b). Model the back nightdress, which has a straight

waistline. Pin back and front together at the sides, and leave open from below the knee at centre back or left side seam. Mark the waistline and side seams and level the hem. Cut a small piece of fabric and model the underarm section. Mark the seamlines.

Pin the widthwise centre of the wide lace to the stand shoulder, extending over the the padded arm. Smooth front over the bust to 1cm ($3/8$") below the upper taped waistline and just over the side panel and pin. Cut off surplus fabric. Smooth and pin the back to the waist in the same way. Pin the narrow lace round the waistline, mitring at centre front. Remove from stand, true up the waistline and open the double skirt fabric out to its full width.

a Stand taped
Padded arm attached to stand at shoulder
C F
Suspend arm
C F
Cut away
b

Nightdress with tucked and lace-panelled bodice

The tucks are stitched to the low waist then fall free to create fullness.

(a) Prepare the tucked sections. Insert a lace panel between them with a further lace panel either side. The width of each panel depends on the width of the lace but in all the five panels should be approximately 30-35cm (12"-14") wide. The length may be from above the knee to the ankle. Add a strip of the main fabric to either side, sufficient to complete as far as the side seams.

NEW TECHNIQUE
Pre-tucked fabric joined to lace panels and main fabric before modelling.

The sides hang straight, 1920's style.

(b) The sleeves are strips of lace, gathered and stitched over tulle to fit the upper armhole. Make three or four frills. Cut the tulle to the same basic shape and wide enough to accommodate the width of the overlapped frills. The neck is bound and the hem overlocked and narrowly hemmed or may be edged with lace.

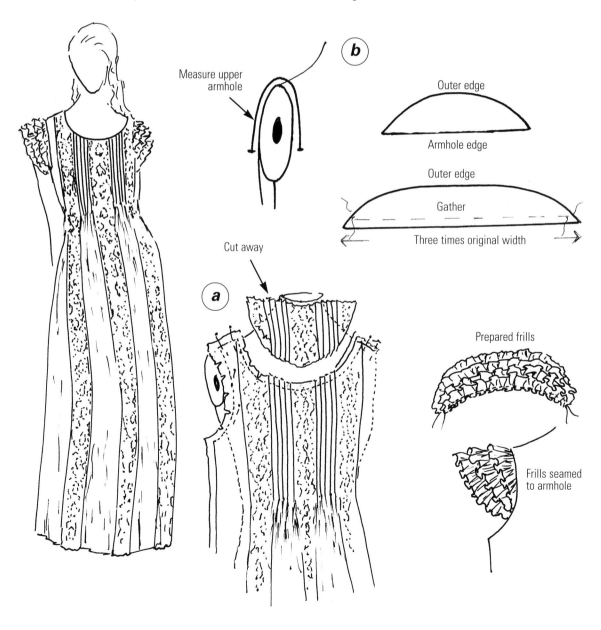

Measure upper armhole

Outer edge

Armhole edge

Outer edge

Gather

Three times original width

Cut away

Prepared frills

Frills seamed to armhole

Asymmetric two-tiered top over French knickers

The knickers are separate (see pages 48-49.) Both tiers of this asymetric top hang from the neckline and are modelled across the whole stand.

Tape design lines onto stand. Cut two lengths of fabric for back and two for front 60cm (24") wide, and to lengths required (cut wider for a fuller flare).

(a) Pin marked fabric centre to centre-front stand seam with a few cemtimetres above strap level to allow for flare. Cut down centre of fabric almost to the design line.

(b) Alllow the fabric to fall towards the centre-front from both left and right sides. Cut along the top edge, snipping and flaring and allowing ease in the neck and armhole edges while flaring the hem until the top edge reaches the underarm at the side seam position. Cut the side seams with a little flare.

(c) How the toile appears before cutting the diagonal hemline.

(d) Pull the fabric at the side seam outwards, keeping the centre-front vertical (it may be helpful if someone else holds the oposite side). Snip the fabric and cut to the opposite side in a long, smooth curve. This may be done on a flat surface if preferred but the effect is judged immediately while cutting on the stand.

Model the back tier in the same way, then the shorter top tiers from the same neckline. Mark seams and notches, remove from stand and true up.

Nightdress with two layers floating from the neckline to deep Van Dyke hem shaping

NEW TECHNIQUE
Modelling in layers on the true bias to achieve a hemline of floating points.

The outer layer has points at centre-front and back and side seams, the underlayer side points and centre back seam. In fine fabrics another layer could be added with points between the two shown. Model the underlayer first, then the outer layer over it. Allow sufficient ease in the low, back neckline for pulling over the head and shoulders.

(a) Tape the upper design lines and shoulder straps onto the stand. Centre seamlines are for guidance only.

(b) Using 112cm (44") wide fabric, cut one length of 224 cm (88") for the under layer and two lengths of 112 cm (44") for the top layer. Threadmark centre front, centre back and true cross. Mark underarm points, centre-front and centre-back.

(c) Lower layer: pin the marked underarm of the fabric to the stand, allowing the thread-mark to fall in line with the stand side seam. The cut edges will be directed towards the centre-back and centre-front.

(d) Smooth front fabric across from U P (underarm point) to strap point, then down to centre-front cutting to 1.5cm (⅝") from seamline, snipping to allow fabric to flare towards the hem and cutting away surplus fabric. The marked centre front should line up with the stand centre-front seamline. Model the left side to the underarm.

(e) Smooth the fabric from both side seams towards the centre-back, following the design line until the weft threads are in line with the stand centre seamline and pin the centre back seam. Surplus fabric can be eased into gathers and elasticated or cut for a smoother fit. Mark seams.

(f) Upper layer: position threadmarked centre-front of fabric in line with the centre-front stand seamline and pin the centre neck point with the cut sides directed to either side. Pin on design line to the straps, then to the underarm, easing to bring the weft threads in line with the stand side seam. Model the back in the same way, following the underlayer. Keep the same amount of ease in both layers. Pin back and front upper layers together at the sides. Mark upper and side seams and notch for matching. The lower points may be sharp or rounded. A crinkly serger finish requires a rounded edge.

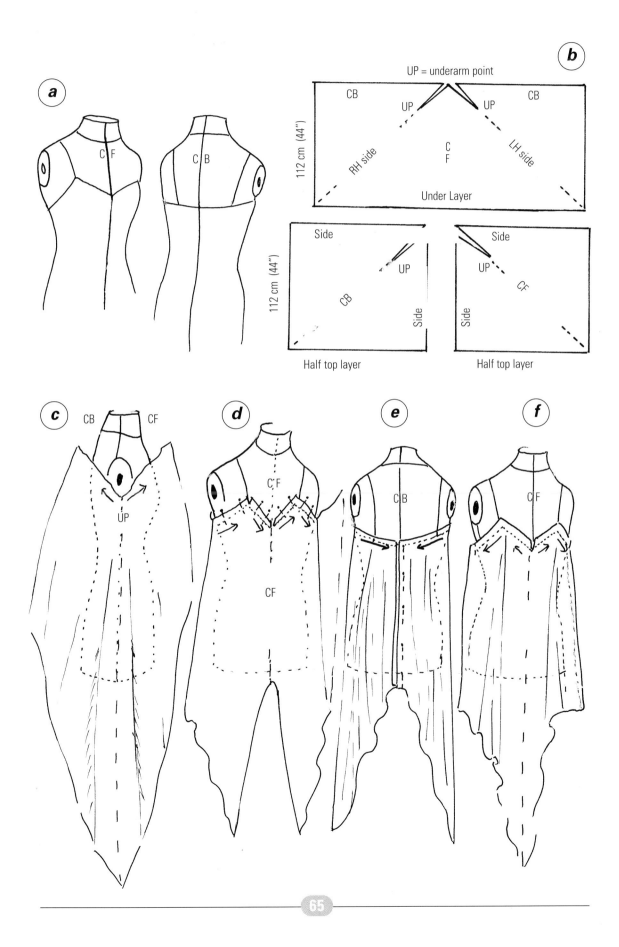

a

b

UP = underarm point

CB   UP   UP   CB

112 cm (44")

RH side   C F   LH side

Under Layer

112 cm (44")

Side   Side

UP   UP

CB   CF

Side   Side

Half top layer   Half top layer

c   CB   CF

UP

d   C F   CF

e   CB

f   CF

Low V-neck, sleeveless lace negligee with cape-effect shoulders

Toile in a similar weight fabric and trace off to make a pattern in the usual way or model fabric directly onto the stand. The shape is simple and relies entirely for its effect on the amount of flare directed into the hem and to the choice of fabric, here a beautiful intricately patterned lace with a lace-trimmed tulle cape joined into the neckline. Suggested nightdress to complement this negligee: follow the same design lines for the neck and armholes, omitting the cape.

Use lace wide enough to create some flare and to go across the entire back negligee without a seam. Cut two full widths at least 20cm (8") longer than the finished length required and split one of them through the vertical centre (for the two fronts). Cut a long strip of tulle for the cape to the depth required and minimum length 150cm (59") to gather and stitch to the neckline. Cut along the roll of fabric if not wide enough.

(a) Tape design lines on stand for the neckline and armhole from upper shoulder to low underarm.
(b) Align the edge of the lace to the centre-front stand seam with 20cm (8") above the side neck point. Cut along the neck edge to the shoulder, trimming fabric to 1.5cm (⁵⁄₈") and snipping every 10cm (4"), allowing fabric to fall into flares at the hem.
(c) Pin from shoulder to underarm, trim fabric to 1.5cm (⁵⁄₈") Flare the side seam.
(d) Back: fold lace in half lengthwise, pin to centre back and shape the neckline along the design line, snipping and flaring to give back fullness equal to the front.
(e) Complete the armhole and side seam. Mark seamlines with a 'fade-away' pen. Leave negligee on stand while modelling the cape.

Single fabric

Double fabric

Cut away

(f) Gather the tulle to fit the negligee neckline. Attach padded arms to the stand and suspend with elastic so that the arms may be bent this way and that to judge the effect. Pin centre of tulle to centre-back neckline, then pin each side round to the centre-front. Mark notches at centre back and side neck points.

(g) Remove from stand, remove gathers and arrange ungathered lace trim to neck and lower edges. Any gap between the lace can be dotted with single motifs.

(h) Re-gather neck edge and check fit on the stand.

Spread flat

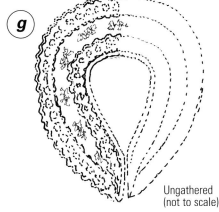

Ungathered
(not to scale)

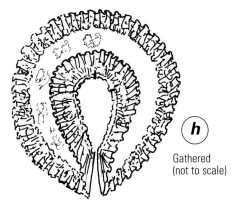

Gathered
(not to scale)

Raglan sleeve wrapover robe with neck ruffle and wide sash

Toile half the back and the right front. Cut two lengths of straight grain fabric to full length of robe plus 5cm (2"). The back width = quarter hip width plus 10cm (4"). Front = quarter hip plus extension to wrap edge (minimum 7.5cm (3") plus 10cm (4"). More width can be introduced into the garment but not more than can be be eased, gathered or pleated effectively into the raglan seam. Mark a line for centre-front on one piece 10cm (4") in from right-hand side of fabric. Cut two pieces of fabric for the sleeve: shoulder to wrist or shorter if making a frill or cuff.

(a) Work on right side of the stand for the back but extend from centre-front into the left-hand side for the front wrap. Attach padded arm to dress stand and suspend from the elbow to allow the arm to bend a little. Pin shoulder pads to raise the shoulders by 13mm (½") adding ease to the completed armhole. Tape neckline and raglan lines. The armhole should be lower, approximately 5cm (2") below the normal underarm point.

(b) Align and pin the marked centre-front of fabric to centre-front stand seamline, smooth from centre to outer edge of wrap and pin at waist. Following the taped neckline, cut surplus fabric to within 1.5cm (⅝") as far as the raglan armhole line.

(c) Smooth remaining fabric fairly loosely across bust point towards the side seam and upwards to the raglan line. Pin small pleats or gathers to provide more width in the front garment and trim seam to within 1.5cm (⅝"). Pin the remainder of the raglan line to the underarm allowing 2.5cm (1") extra fabric at the side seam for easy arm movement and extra bust width.

(d) Model back robe from centre back seam, shaping back neckline. Continue along raglan line, easing fabric fairly loosely to armhole as required but omit gathers or pleats which are unnecessary and unattractive at the back. Leave 2.5cm (1") extra fabric at the side seam. Pin side seams together. Mark seamlines and balance marks.

DESIGN NOTE
The raglan sleeve extends into the bodice section of the neckline at back and front and is known as a 'grown-on' sleeve.

(e) Model a sleeve on the padded arm with straight grain from shoulder to wrist. Finished sleeve width should be between 15 -18cm (38 - 45") for comfort. Pin the front section from shoulder point to hem leaving 18cm (7") above for the shoulder section. Pin the underarm seam from wrist to underarm.

(f) Follow the raglan line to pin and trim the front seamline from underarm to neck, then return to the shoulder point to shape shoulder to neck. Model the back sleeve in the same way. Mark all seamlines, add notches for matching seams and marking pleats or eased sections. Remove from the stand, true up and trace pieces onto paper.

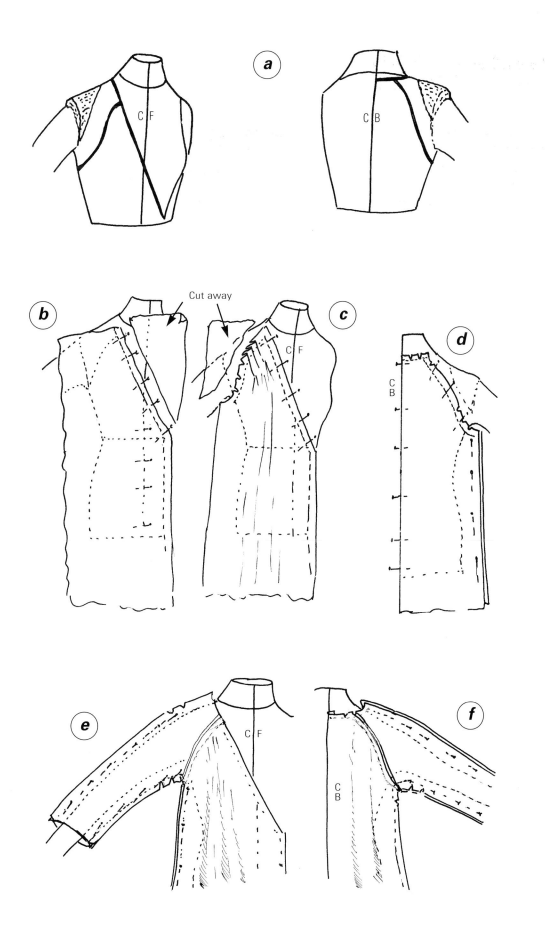

a

b

c

Cut away

d

e

f

C F

C B

Neck and sleeve ruffles and wide sash for robe

Ungathered neck ruffle (f)

(a) Tape outer edge of ruffle on dress stand in a smooth curve. Following neckline and outer curve, model the back section to the shoulder seam, then the front. Mark neckline, outer edge, centre-back and side neck notch. (b) Remove from stand and trace onto paper. Join together at the shoulder. As it is, this pattern can be used for a smooth collar with no ruffles (c).

(d) Mark slash lines at 10cm (4") intervals on the paper from neckline to outer edge. Cut from the outer edge to the neckline but try not to cut the neckline itself. Spread the outer line to obtain a longer edge. The ruffle will curl into a snail shape.

Gathered neck ruffle (g)

(e) Follow the above directions but cut through the traced collar pattern and spread both edges. Test in appropriate fabric to judge the effect. The robe collar should be cut from double fabric and bound to the neck edge. Use a lighter weight fabric for the undercollar. Neck ruffles in very fine fabrics may be cut from single thickness fabric and overlocked to give a crisp outer edge.

Sleeve ruffle (h)

Cut paper to the length required by the whole sleeve width. Mark slash lines and spread in the same way as the neck ruffle.

Robe sash (i)

Cut fabric to length and width required. A wide sash should be a minimum of 2.30cm (90") long by 15cm (6") wide.

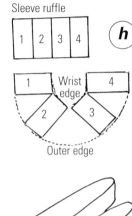

Sleeve ruffle

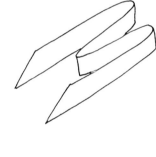

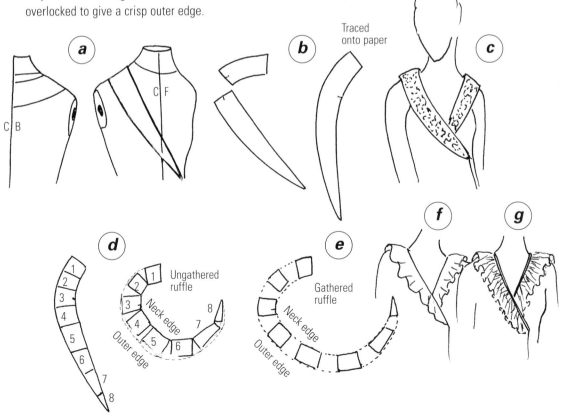

Modelling pyjama shorts and long trousers

Pyjama shorts and trousers should be loose enough to sleep in without discomfort. In woven fabrics the seat length is increased by at least 5.5cm (2¼") and the width by at least a third. Model the shorts toile as for French knickers (page 48) allowing more garment width through waist to lower edge but keeping the side seams straight instead of flared. Additional length

can be introduced by tacking a large fold horizontally in the fabric before modelling or by adding it to the paper pattern. The insertion takes place just below the hip level. The following flat pattern cutting instructions show how to adjust a trousers block for pyjamas.

Outline culotte slip or a basic trouser block to length required. Draw vertical lines for widening the pattern and horizontal slash lines for lengthening the torso as shown. Cut through lines and spread. It is quicker to outline part of the block then move it sideways to widen and upwards to lengthen between crotch and hip level. Then pivot from the back side-seam to increase the centre-back length by a further 3cm (1³⁄₈").

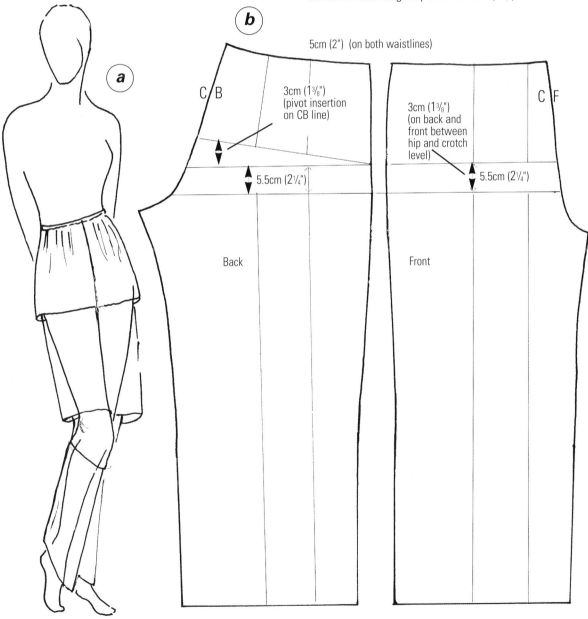

Classic styling in nightwear: strap front opening

This page shows design ideas for pyjama tops and an all-in-one pyjama which incorporate various strap front openings. The techniques can be applied to most basic silhouettes for pyjama tops, nightdresses, and leisure and sportswear. The designs are meant to be fun to wear, to be seen by friends, suitable for young people away from home, perhaps at college and for pyjama parties. However the classic features are suitable for any age group.

Variations of the strap front opening: from left to right

a) Strap front opening in a slash, set into a plastron front. The visible edge only needs a facing and the underwrap needs a joined-on strap.

(b) Two-piece strap front as described on page 73, set into a yoked bodice.

(c) Mock strap opening. This is a normal buttonstand opening ending in a horizontal seamline, giving the appearance of a strap opening. The facing may be on the inside of the garment and topstitched, or sewn onto the outside, forming a decorative facing.

(d) One-piece top and trouser pyjama. A normal buttonstand ending in a vertical seam gives the appearance of a strap, emphasised by the stitching securing the facing. All-in-one garments require extra length (see page 77 for a shortie all-in-one pyjama).

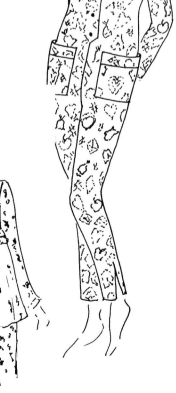

Classic styling in nightwear

There are many variations of the classic strap opening. In its simplest form shown below it can be of various lengths and widths, of self or of contrasting fabric, left plain or with piped or bound edges, and have straight or curved edges at the neckline.

The strap can also be joined to the neck facing and applied to either the inside or the outside of a garment, which is particularly effective in contrast fabric. See page 74 for this type of neckline.

Instead of a rectangular gap, the opening can also be made in a slash, when only the left-hand side has a strap to take the buttons.

The strap opening effect can also be achieved by the 'mock strap'. A normal buttonstand as added and the lower end of the opening enclosed in a yokeline seam. This also makes it possible to add more ease into the body of the garment in the form of gathers, flare, tucks and pleats and gives more scope for designers to create interesting collections. Necklines do not need to be collarless and simple collars such as the Peter Pan and Mandarin collar are quite common.

For a simple front strap construct the pattern by flat pattern cutting as follows: draw two rectangles, one for the overlap, one for the underlap, each the length of the opening by twice the strap width. Mark a fold line through the centre of each. On the overlap mark vertical buttonholes through the centre. On the underlap mark button positions. Add 1cm seam allowance to all edges. Patterns are shown for a straight and a pointed end.

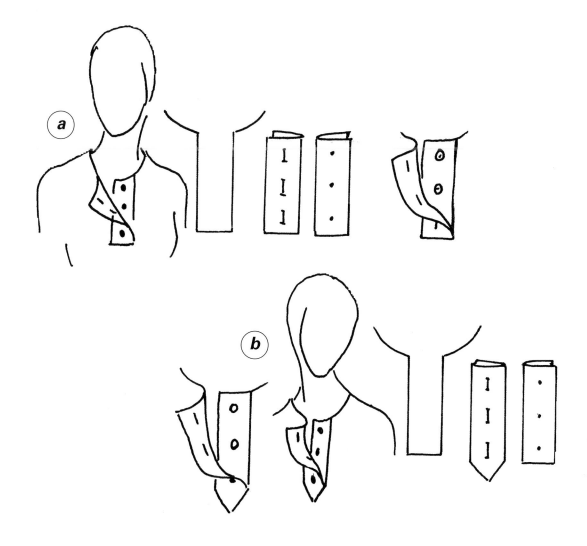

Classic styling in nightwear

Strap opening and decorative facing in contrast fabric

Cut two lengths of straight grain fabric 76cm (30"). Width = one whole width of 112cm (44") wide fabric. Cut front strip of straight grain contrasting fabric 25cm (10") wide by side neck to length of opening plus 5cm (2"). For the back facing cut fabric 33cm (13") wide by 7.5cm (3") deep. Each sleeve band takes 30cm (12") x sleeve width.

(a) Attach padded arm to the dress stand and suspend arm. Pin shoulder pads to raise the shoulders by 13mm (½") to add ease for arm movement. Tape a new shoulder seam 13mm (½") towards the front from side neckpoint through centre-shoulder to wrist.

(b) Tape two parallel lines 4cm (1½") apart from nape at centre-back to side-neck point then curve across the front to 2cm (¾") beyond centre-front stand seamline. Continue vertically to length required.

Neck facing and strap

(c) Pin back contrast fabric with straight grain to centre-back. Shape back neckline to shoulder, snipping to the seamline and trimming fabric to 1.5cm (⅝"). Lay fabric over centre-front neck and pin along both taped lines. Follow neck curve to the shoulder. Pin and trim shoulder seam. Mark the seamlines and vertical buttonhole positions through the strap centre. Remove toile from stand, true lines and curves and trace onto pattern paper (d).

(e) Pyjama front: pin fabric to centre-front stand seamline with sufficient fabric above to reach beyond the shoulder. Anchor pin remaining fabric to free hands. Pin fabric to lower taped neckline, snipping and trimming until the shoulder is reached. Allow fabric to hang loose from shoulder to hem and pin the shoulder seam. Continue along the upper arm to the length required. Cut away surplus fabric.

(f) Model back pyjama in the same way, following the lower taped neckline. Bring remaining fabric together at underarm and pin the seamline, linking it in a curved seam. The armhole should extend fairly low, approximately 5cm (2") below the normal underarm point. Do not shape the pyjama in at the waist. It should hang straight. Mark all seams and add notches to sleeve and bodice for accurate matching.

(g) Make a double sleeve band to attach to the sleeve end and turn back to form a cuff.

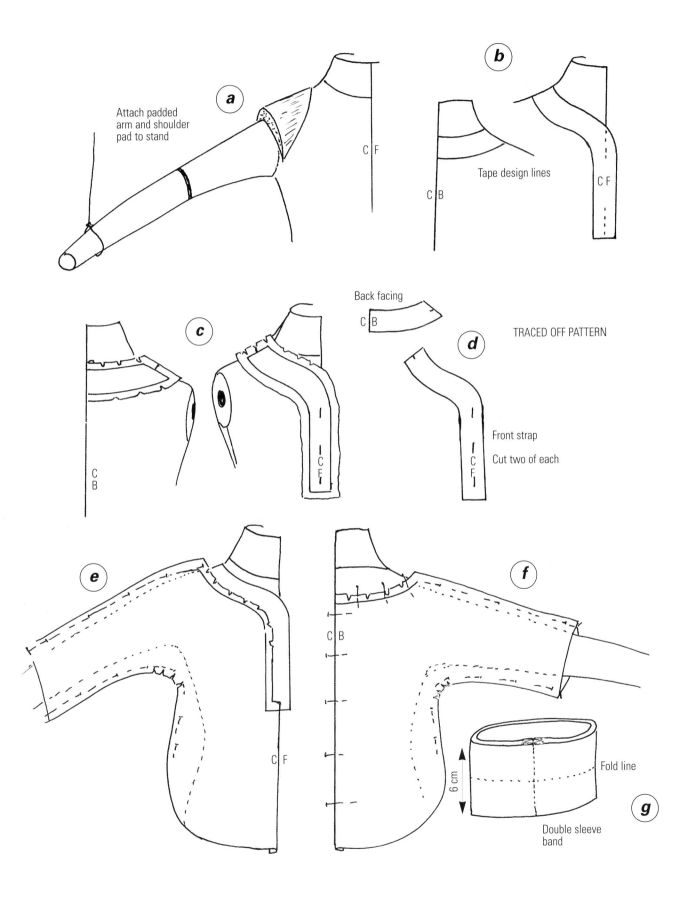

a Attach padded arm and shoulder pad to stand

C F

b Tape design lines

C B

C F

c

C B

C F

Back facing

C B

d TRACED OFF PATTERN

Front strap

Cut two of each

C F

e

C F

f

C B

g Fold line

6 cm

Double sleeve band

(a) Mark a slash line 2cm (¾") beyond the centre-front and mark buttonhole positions on the centre-front stand seamline. The button strap must be of double fabric and a facing is needed for the buttonhole side. The same pattern can be used to cut the interfacing. The buttonhole facing and upper side of the button strap could be cut in one piece with a separate shorter piece to back the button strap. This strap is shown in a plastron front, which is simply a large, curved yoke.

(b) Model the back bodice and construct a normal buttonstand at centre front. Mark seams, shoulder and side seam notches. Remove toile from the stand, true up and trace seamlines onto pattern paper. Draw on the back neck facing and front neck and buttonstand facing. Trace off the facing separately.

Strap opening in a slash

Cut two for buttonstrap

Cut one facing for buttonhole strap

C F

C F

Cut 2cm beyond centre-front

Plan understrap

FRONT

Mock strap opening in a seam

C F

CF

BACK

C B

C B

C B

C B

Introducing pleats:
yoked playsuit pyjamas

All-in-one pyjama

When bodice and trousers of any length are combined, the garment will need extra length in addition to the through trunk measurement to allow for bending and stretching. This is even more so in sleepwear when movement is involuntary. Check the full trunk length (see camiknickers, page 56). For the smooth jersey pyjamas on page 75, keep the legs narrower and omit the yoke and pleats of the pyjama below.

The yoke and pockets should be cut double in self fabric or contrast. Leave the pyjama sleeveless for summer wear. A low, comfortable armhole is comfortable for sleepwear. For long sleeves, use the padded arm separately to model a one-piece sleeve, fairly loose at the armhole, then pin the arm to the stand to complete the sleeve-head shaping. The long front edges need a facing and the armholes can be faced or bound.

(a) Tape square neckline, yoke line and leg length. Cut two lengths of fabric on straight grain.
Length = yokeline to leg length plus 13cm (5") by ¼ bust width (hip if wider) plus 20cm (4"). Cut two peices approximately 51cm (20") wide X 28cm (11") deep for the yokes.

(b) Model the back and front yoke sections on fabric straight grain, extending the centre-front to form the buttonstand. Mark seams and notches.

(c) Model the lower sections in the same way as the camiknickers on page 57, extending fabric beyond centre seamlines to allow for crotch shaping. Lower the crotch level and introduce fullness for body movement with pleats or gathers into the yokeline. Cut legs to length required.

DESIGN NOTE

Garments with unbroken lines from wrist to wrist across the body call for fabrics over 120cm (47") wide. When using narrower fabrics the problem can be solved by using seams at centre-back or front. Another device is to separate the kimono sleeve from the body and create a dropped shoulder. A simple dropped sleeve style can be adapted from the previous kimono bodice and can be used for short or long styles.

Dropped sleeve styles

V neck shortie shirt robe with dropped shoulder sleeves

Attach padded arm and shoulder pad to the stand and tape a V neck and buttonstand on the dress stand. Cut back and front fabric to length required, here above knee.

(a) Work as for the kimono pyjama top on page 74 but introduce some flare from the shoulder to give more body room and end the sleeve above the elbow or to full length if required. The facings can be topstitched from the right side of the garment or sewn to the outside as a decorative facing and a trim inserted, as in this example, repeated at sleeve ends and pockets.

(b) Draw the dropped shoulder line onto the sleeve section below the shoulder in a slightly curved line (this can be done at the pattern stage). Mark seams and notches and remove toile from stand. Cut off the sleeve section, trace toile seamlines onto pattern paper and join to make a one-piece sleeve. The seam will be in the underarm position.

C B

a

C F

Draw on dropped shoulder line

C B

C F

Sleeve

b

Join

Nightwear designs

Nightwear should be as enjoyable to design, make and wear as clothes for any other occasion. It need not be limited to a couple of simple nightdresses, or pyjamas and a robe, but teamed with matching or contrasting jackets, bathroom hold-all bags and bedroom mules. See pages 80-81 for the mules pattern and instructions.

e) Round yoke, long sleeved shortie robe over short, tiered cotton nightdress.

(b) Quilted sleeveless jerkin over long-sleeved pyjamas.

c) Shortie robe over crop top vest and culotte pyjamas.

d) Cut-away tabard with Mandarin collar, front loop and button fastening and split sides over all-in-one blouson pyjama.

e) Shoulder fastening, split side tunic over long-sleeved jersey top and matador pyjama trousers.

Matching mules for nightwear

Mules have soft soles and can be padded with high density foam. Use purchased soles or the suede side of leather, thick felt or other strong but lightweight material as a base. The upper section may be an Eastern toe-loop with a beaded motif secured to the sole by straps, loops with cords or ribbons, or fabric shaped to the sides of the sole and fastening with Velcro or laced through eyelet holes.

(a) Draw round an existing slipper to make a pattern for the sole (pattern on page 81).

(b) Use this pattern with no seam allowances to cut the base sole and the foam. Measure the upper part of the foot for the upper sections, which will be wider than the sole pattern. Cut two uppers for each foot. Use the sides of the soles as a guide and round off the edges which will overlap (shown in (e) and (f).

(c) Cut a double layer of pyjama fabric for the inner sole and upper mule sections and add 1.5 - 2 cm (⅝"- ¾") seam allowances all round, depending on the thickness of the foam layer. Right sides together, machine each pair of inner soles together leaving a gap of about 10cm (4") open along the instep. Trim turnings, turn through and slip the foam soles inside. Close the gap by hand or machine stitching.

Make the upper sections as follows:

Each mule has two upper sections which can be laced up or Velcroed to fasten.

Interline the uppers with strong interfacing or a layer of wadding.
Machine round three edges and trim, leaving the outer sole edge open.
Turn through to the outside. Press and topstitch the machined seam and close the opening on the fitting line. Make eyelet holes or attach Velcro.

(d) Wrong side up, position the seam allowance of the uppers onto the completed inner soles and machine 1cm (⅜") from outer edge and again, close to the edge.

(e) Position the underneath of the inner sole onto the base sole. Fabric glue can be used to stick the two together and this can be reinforced by machine stitching through all layers. Laces can be purchased, made from cord-covered rouleau or coloured cords.

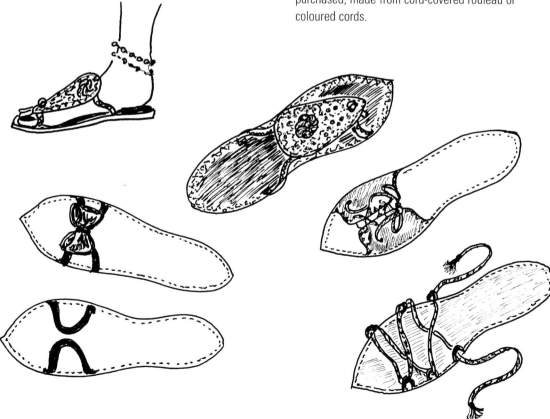

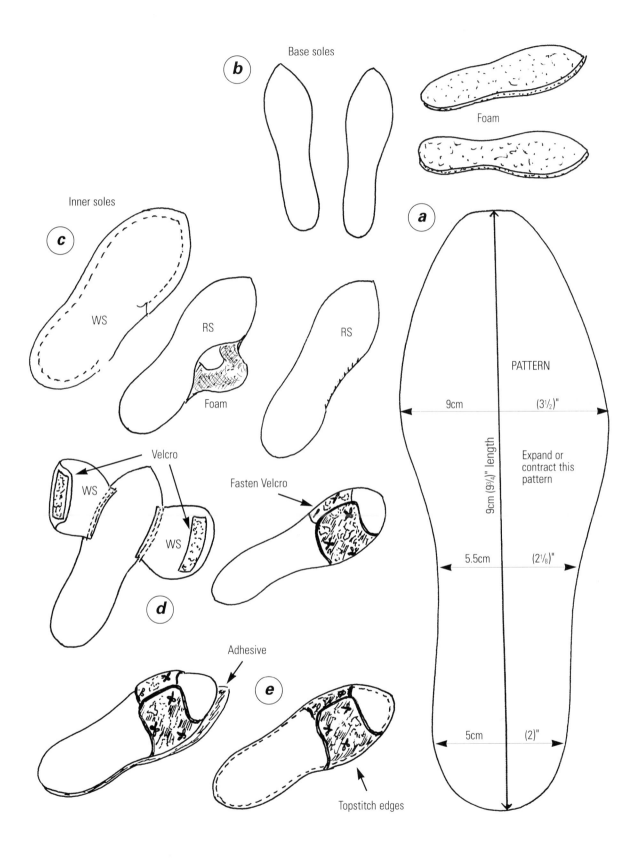

Base soles

b

Foam

Inner soles

c

WS

RS

Foam

RS

a

PATTERN

9cm   (3½)"

9cm (9¾)" length

Expand or
contract this
pattern

5.5cm   (2⅛)"

Velcro

WS

Fasten Velcro

WS

WS

d

5cm   (2)"

Adhesive

e

Topstitch edges

Underwear as eveningwear

Body beneath the suit

Day into evening

Slip off the tailored jacket to reveal a glamorous body ready for evening. The all-in-one stretch bodies described on pages 40-41 are perfect foundations for day or eveningwear and can be worn under town dresses, executive suits, evening or partywear.

Technological advances combining elastomeric fibres with fabrics suitable for outerwear followed by consequent designer innovation have taken the 'body' into another dimension. The 'body' is now on show as party and evening wear. The black lace and jersey body on this page takes it one step further and could be described as a vest and brief with built-in bra and long sleeves. It could double equally well under a suit by day or as an attractive top teamed with long skirts or trousers with a cummerband for evening.

Tape the design lines on a lingerie or swimwear stand. Include the armhole, which for stretch fabric can be raised 1.5cm (5/8") above the normal armhole position. Model the bust section first, in jersey, stretching the fabric slightly to the curves. Any surplus fabric should be eased into the under-bust seam below the bust point.

The centre body can be modelled with side seams only, or panel lines introduced for more control. A separate gusset is constructed and added to the back body with the gusset opening towards the front.

The pattern for the padded arm on page 90 is made exactly to arm measurements and can be used as a close-fitting sleeve pattern for stretch fabrics. Add 1cm (3/8") seam allowance.

Adjustable fastening

Lower front 'body'

Lower back 'body'

Back crotch seam

Adjustable fastening

Waspie or evening cummerband?

Just as a wide band of elastomeric fabric worn next to the skin will cinch the waist and control flesh in the midriff and stomach areas, the same effect can be achieved by transforming it into a cummerband or the midriff of a dress, as illustrated below. The velvet midriff section is stiched to the bodice and skirt seams and the lacing is purely decorative. Made up as a separate garment it would need to be boned to prevent it riding up but could have an authentic laced opening.

In this dress the velvet 'waspie' midriff section is made up before joining to the skirt and draped upper bodice. Model the midriff panels on the dress stand and mark the seams and notches. Loops for the lacing are sewn into the front panel seams. In a dress with shoulder seams boning the midriff section would not be necessary. In this strapless dress it is essential.

Separate laced waspie

Tape the side seams and panel lines onto the stand but disregard the centre-front stand seam, taping the 'centre-front' edges 2.5cm (1") or more from the stand centre seamline to enable the lacing to be pulled together without overlapping - 5cm (2") in all. This amount is recommended for normal daywear but could be doubled for a next-to-the-skin waspie.

Boning is recommended on side seams, panel lines, centre-back and each side of centre-front. To avoid the ridges made by casings, line the whole garment and machine 'channels' through which the bones will be slotted.

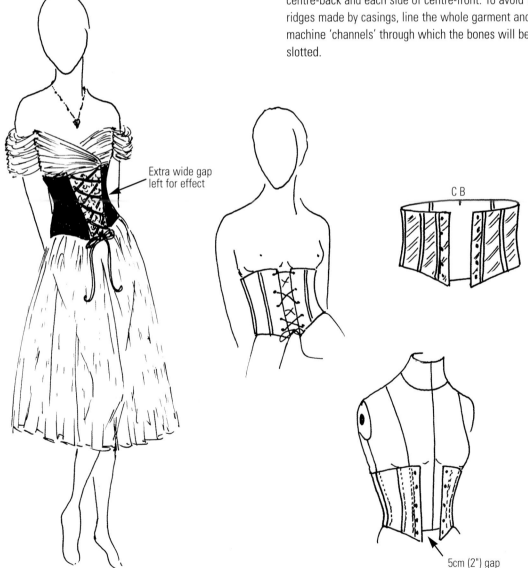

Extra wide gap left for effect

C B

5cm (2") gap

Corset or bustier as eveningwear

The old-fashioned lace-up corset has taken on a new lease of life as the modern 'bustier', shown here in lace panels divided by satin ribbon bands over the bone casings and with back lacing. The separate sleeves are modelled on the padded arm.

Work on the right hand side of the stand. Tape the panel lines, upper and lower edges. Tape the centre back 2.5 cm (1") from each side - 5cm (2") in all, in the same way as the front lace-up waspie on page 83. The upper front is not modelled as high as a strapless bra but cuts across the breasts in a straighter line.

Model the centre-front panel first, snipping fabric to the panel seamline over the bust curves, then in the order suggested, working from centre-front to side, then from centre-back to side seam. Shape the lower edge, mark and notch the seams and remove from the stand. True lines and transfer to paper. If a day-wear dress stand is used, tighten the upper bodice to body size by taking a little off the seams over the bust, reduce the side seams for a tighter fit and shape the midriff seams under the bust as described in the bust circle on page 30. Measure the panel lines to estimate the length of satin ribbon need to make the bone

casings, which are machined to the outer bustier and the bones slotted through before the lower edge is bound to match the upper edge.

Separate sleeve or glove

Use stretch lace to match the bustier and pin to the padded arm with one inner seamline. The top is bound with stretch satin binding or ribbon to match the bodice bone casings. The wrist may be extended and stretched to cover part of the hand and thumb.

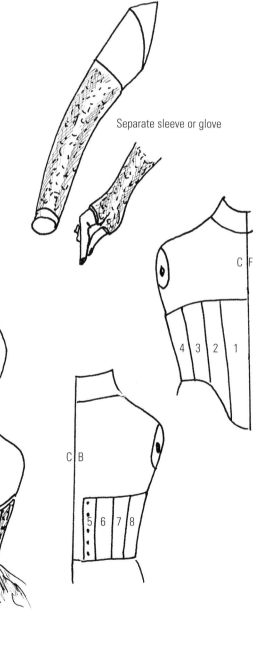

Separate sleeve or glove

Little black vest and metallic vest

The traditional scoop neck, wide shouldered, sleeveless, hip-length knit vest was perhaps the least inspiring garment in any woman's wardrobe and only purchased for warm winterwear under more attractive clothing. Now elevated to both day and eveningwear it has become an indispensable wardrobe item to be teamed with skirts and trousers.

Two variations of the vest are featured below. The 'little black vest' in clingy jersey is the perfect foil for fabrics in exotic colours for both day and eveningwear. Shortened to high hip level, it can be worn inside or outside skirts and trousers. Above the waist it becomes a 'crop-top.'

The stretch metallic, fine-knit cropped vest has dainty straps, a wrapover bodice designed to be worn bra-less and a self-coloured embroidered midriff section. The outer edges are turned under double and hemmed with a stretch stitch, giving a border effect. Make sure the stretch fabric used will stretch and recover to pull over the head. If an opening becomes necessary use the narrowest possible 'snap-all' tape - fine but strong fastener suitable for lingerie and other delicate garments.

(a) Scoop neck vest

Model in two pieces, front and back across the whole stand, with a high side seam and snug armhole. The outer edges are all single layer hems.

(b) Metallic crop top vest

Both sides of the stand can be taped. Model only one wrapover section. Start from centre-front, leaving enough fabric for the wrap beyond centre-front and smoothing above and round outer bust curve to the side seam. Ease in any surplus fabric below the bust point. Complete the wrap.

Model the upper-back section across both sides of the stand. Take a straight, wide band of embroidered fabric and pin it all round the midriff, starting and finishing at the left-hand side seam. Mark and notch seams. Measure for shoulder straps. Remove from stand.

Little black vest

Metallic fabric vest

a

b

Slip into the evening shift

The 'shift', once a simply cut chemise or camisole, later developed into the slip and made a come-back as a 'tube' dress in the 1950s, worn quite straight with a simple neckline which could be slipped over the head. When tubular fabric (no seams) is available in appropriate fabrics, only the neckline and armholes have to be considered. Any such simply-cut dress could be said to derive from the original undergarment. The more

recent classic slip (see page 52) with its pleated under-bust line and bias-cut skirt has evolved as a classic dress for special occasion clothes. With the minimum of shaping, yet well-cut, its success lies in the choice of fabric and decoration. The same basic pattern can be used over and over with simple changes of neckline, without having to re-draft or re-model from scratch. Narrow fabric widths restrict the length of bias-cut garments but the introduction of design seams only become necessary when longer garments are required.

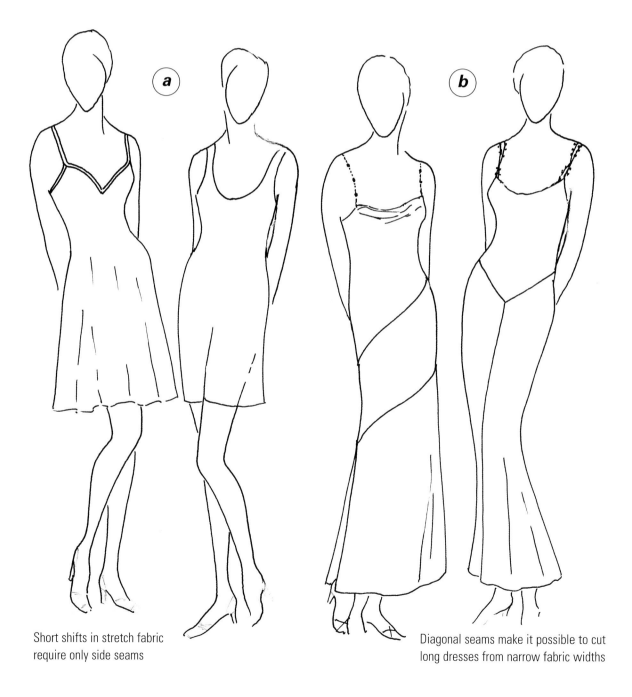

Short shifts in stretch fabric require only side seams

Diagonal seams make it possible to cut long dresses from narrow fabric widths

Camisoles for party and eveningwear

The versatile camisole has a role to play from morning to night as underwear, daywear, nightwear and in suitable fabrics, eveningwear. Evening tops based on the camisole can 'mix and match' effectively, adding variety to a limited number of skirts or trousers for special occasions.

Camisoles take very little material, rarely more than 50cm (half a yard) making it possible to select quite expensive fabrics for relatively little outlay per garment. When off-cuts and remnants of expensive luxury fabrics are available the cost is even less. In small amounts quite exotic colourful fabrics are successful when they contrast with skirt or trousers in a solid colour. In plain fabrics, this simple garment is transformed by the addition of beads, sequins or embroidered motifs or weaves such as velvet and brocade, and can be further enhanced with the addition of fine beaded chains or strings of diamonté as shoulder straps, as in (c) below. Camisoles in all-over beading or sequins sparkle under artificial light and provide the focal point of an outfit.

Like its underwear equivalent, the evening camisole is looser than a vest and can be worn over a strapless bra or body, or be worn bra-less. Most camisoles have straps or narrow shoulders which should not have to argue with the straps of undergarments.

The camisoles sketched below are designed on simple lines. It is the fabric which lifts them out of the ordinary.

(a) Black sequin-covered stretch fabric.
(b) Jet-beaded raised motifs and jet-bugle beaded upper edge and straps on black organza.
(c) Embroidered organza with beaded chain edgings and straps.

Negligee or lace evening coat?

This simply-cut lace evening coat in a heavy lace such as guipure and worn over matching lace or sheer pleated trousers makes stunning eveningwear, yet in a finer lace would be reminiscent of a negligee and a suitable design to be worn over a nightdress. The trousers can be teamed with a body or made with built-in briefs and worn with a strapless top, camisole or vest. The open-fronted coat is designed to show off what is worn beneath but can be modelled to the centre-front and fastened. The sleeves may be long or short and the silhouette slightly flared but is also effective cut straight with long side splits to give some movement.

Both these long pants can be worn as special occasion clothes. Another alternative is to model stretch lace tights with a built-in pantie in a fine-weight but dense fabric. Follow the directions for tights on page 45 and model them over the pantie, which will be joined to the tights at the waist.

The organdie trousers also have a built-in pantie of slightly thicker fabric joined at the waist with decorative lingerie elastic in the same way as the culotte slip on page 58. To create the wider leg, flare can be added equally to the side and the inner leg seams.

Choose a good weight lace edging to finish all the outer coat edges to give some weight to the garment. Lace with a little sparkle worked into the motifs lifts this design from lingerie to eveningwear.

Puss-in-Boots embroidered ankle-length tights or stockings

Wear as tights with a mini skirt or as stockings with a longer skirt.

Use ready-embroidered stretch knit fabric. If you do not have a legged stand, use the leg block on this page for stockings or added to the nether block for tights and make a paper pattern. Tights have inner and outer leg seams, the stockings a single seam at the centre-back of the leg. For very stretchy fabric make a strap for the instep as seen in stirrup pumps. For the tights instruction see page 45.

Leg block (from the groin - the highest part of the top leg - to ankle.) The block is constructed exactly to body size. No tolerance is needed if stretch fabric is used. Depending on the stretch and recovery of the fabric the pattern may need narrowing by folding vertically through the centre. The seam is positioned at centre-back leg.

Measurements needed: upper thigh, knee, calf and ankle girth; lengths = from groin to thigh, to knee, to calf, to ankle (size 12 measurements quoted). Thigh = midway between groin and knee.

Draw a vertical line for centre-front leg and construct horizontal lines across at the various lengths. Measure out to each side from centre: half the measures of groin, thigh, knee, calf, ankle. Join the points, curving in towards the knee, out to the calf and in towards the ankle.

LEG BLOCK

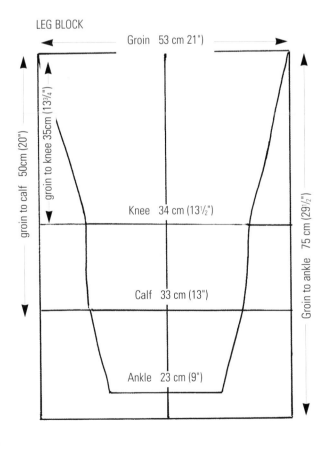

Groin 53 cm 21")

groin to calf 50cm (20")

groin to knee 35cm (13¾")

Knee 34 cm (13½")

Calf 33 cm (13")

Ankle 23 cm (9")

Groin to ankle 75 cm (29½")

STIRRUP PANTS

Strap

Making a padded arm for the dress stand

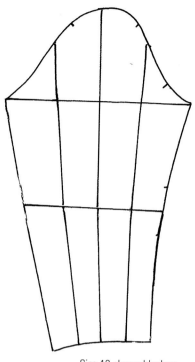

Size 12 sleeve block or
commercial pattern minus
seam allowances

One of the greatest boons to dress designers would be a flexible dress stand with attached arms so that garments could be modelled and draped on a replica of the human figure. Most stands, however, are quite rigid and only suitable for detachable arms, which are available from stand manufacturers. Arms which are attached to the stand by magnets keep the arm very close to the stand. i.e., it is not possible to lift the arm sideways. The instructions below are for adjusting a block or commercial paper pattern to make a detachable padded arm which can be pinned to the stand and bent in all directions. It is also useful for the separate modelling of sleeve designs.

The chart shows body measurements plus tolerances for sleeve patterns. Use only the body measurements for a padded arm. Use the additional measurements for sleeve patterns.

Size 12 pattern	Body size	Tolerance	Total	Increment per size
Outer arm length	58cm (22⅞")	–	58cm (22⅛")	0.9cm (⅜")
Bicep	26.5cm (10½")	5cm (2")	31.5cm (12½")	1.8cm (¾")
Elbow	25 cm (9⅞")	5cm (2")	30cm (11⅞")	1.8cm (¾")
Wrist	16cm (6¼") 2cm (⅞")	6.5cm (2½")* 18cm (7⅛")	22.5cm (9") 0.8cm (⅜")	– –
Armhole	42.7 (16¾")	includes ease**	42.7 cm (16¾")	2cm (¾")

*   6.5cm (2½") tolerance is required for pulling over hand. With a sleeve opening at the wrist, this may be reduced to 2cm (⅞")
** sewing ease for curved sleevehead seam (see lower page 17).
    Instructions for a body size 12 arm. For other sizes consult the size chart on page 9. Use a size 12 sleeve block. If using a commercial pattern cut off the seam allowances.

1. Trace the sleeve onto separate pattern paper on the fitting (sewing) line, i.e., no seam allowance. Rule a line through centre of sleeve.
2. Check sleeve length from crown to wrist 58cm (22⅛").
3. On underarm line, position half bicep measure each side of centre line 13.25cm (11¹⁄₁₆").
4. At elbow level, position half elbow measure each side of centre line 12.5cm (5").
5. At wrist level, position half wrist measure each side of centre line 8cm (6⅛").
6. Join these new points for inner sleeve seam.
7. Reduce crown height to one third of armhole measure 14.2cm(5⅝").
8. Divide horizontal lines into quarters and draw vertical lines through these points. Add notches.
9. Draw the shoulder flap and the shoulder and wrist closures as shown.

(a) Draw the circles for armhole and wrist and the shoulder flap. Add 1cm (³⁄₈") seam allowance to all edges.

(b) Add 1cm (³⁄₈") seam allowances to the padded arm pattern. Cut out in firm calico or linen, from a single layer for one right arm, or from double fabric for a pair of arms.

(c) Mark (or machine narrow black tape to) the centre line, underarm line, elbow line, ease notches on sleeve seam and armhole notches onto the right side of the cut sleeve. Mark the seam allowances on the wrist and shoulder circles and the shoulder flap.

(d) Run a machine easing thread between the notches on the sleevehead and between the notches on the back seamline of the sleeve (or make a dart at the elbow).

(e) On the wrong side, machine the sleeve seam from underarm to wrist and press the seam open. Pin and sew the wrist circle to the narrow end of the sleeve.

(f) Shoulder flap: with right sides together, machine the curved edge. Trim seam and turn to right side. Press. Tack the raw edges together. On the right side of the sleevehead, position the flap between the notches, pin and machine on seamline.

(g) With the flap remaining on the outside, stuff the arm with wadding. Pin and hand sew the top arm circle to close the arm.

(h) The arm may be attached to the stand with pins, or Velcro can be machined to the underside of the flap and the other side of the Velcro fixed to the stand shoulder.

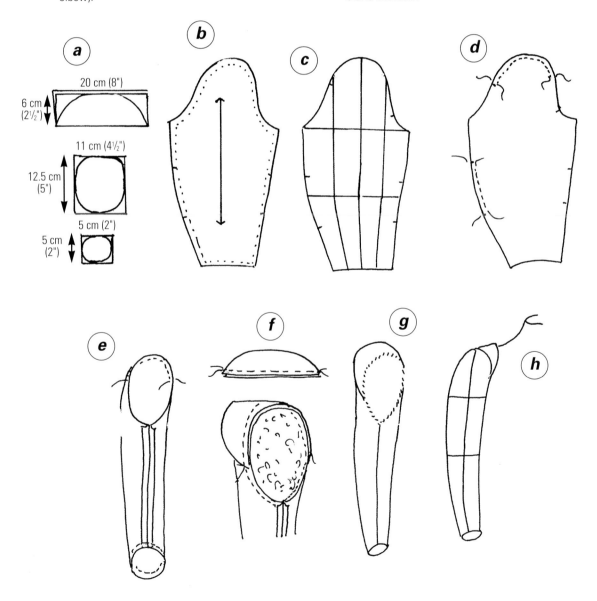

Bra blocks

The instructions for making bras or referring to the bra sections of bodies discuss the reduction of body tolerance in the garment to ensure a very close fit (pages 32-44). To make a collection of basic bra blocks for future use and for grading to larger or smaller sizes, model the single-dart bra and the variously placed seamed bras, transfer the toiles to paper but omit the seam allowances and grain lines, both of which depend on the type of fabric being used. Make more permanent blocks by copying the paper blocks in firm card or plastic. Use these basic bra blocks in the same way as other blocks to develop new designs by changing seam and dart positions. The larger amount of surface in the long-line bra on page 38 offers even more design possibilities.

Grading the bra blocks

Bra manufacturers will- ideally - invest in the full range of lingerie stands in the bust sizes for which they design, an investment beyond the scope of most patternmakers outside large professional workrooms. Lingerie stands may be padded up for larger sizes and this is recommended for individual clients outside the standard size range. To grade up or down in standard sizes it is quicker to use the flat pattern cutting method shown below.

Bra grading involves two adjustments: girth and cup size

Girth: the under bust level (rib cage) differs by 5cm (2") per size and can be adjusted by increasing or decreasing by 1.25cm (½") on the back and the front of the half pattern at the underarm or forward seam.

Cup size: constructing the bra cup using the measurements in the standard size chart (page 12-13) or a dress bodice block, followed by the tolerance reductions described on page 30 will produce an 'A' cup (see cup sizes on page 29). To increase cup size add 1cm (⅜") horizontally at the bust level, in line with the bust points. This increases the vertical height of the bra cup. The same amount must also be added to the back bra section at the side so that the forward side seams are the same length. In the vertical seam bra below, remember to re-join the sections after inserting the 1cm (⅜"). Use the same amounts per size to grade to size 10 and 8.

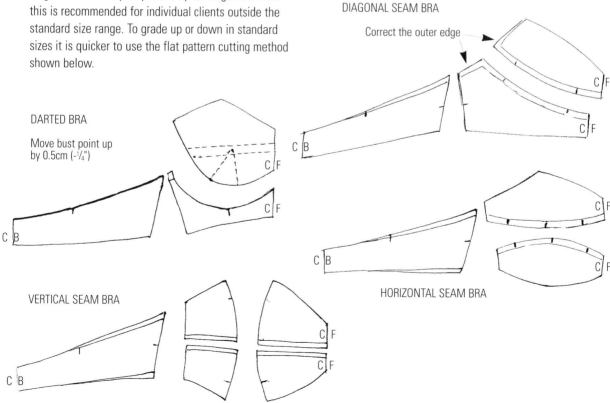

DARTED BRA

Move bust point up by 0.5cm (-¼")

VERTICAL SEAM BRA

DIAGONAL SEAM BRA

Correct the outer edge

HORIZONTAL SEAM BRA

Blocks

Comfort gusset

The 'comfort' block is for nether garments with a lengthwise seam between the legs
(such as French knickers) and is made up separately and stitched in after the garment is made. It protects the body from seam friction and at the same time protects the seam from wear. This gusset is cut double from soft fabric and its edges overlocked before catching it in position to cover the crotch seam.

Gusset block for nether garments

The gusset pattern is provided as a guide for garments which do not have an extended gusset as in tights, culottes and French knickers, where the centre seams continue until they meet at the inner-leg seam.
There being no seams in the centre crotch area, it is smooth and comfortable to wear and particularly suitable for close-fitting garments such as briefs and bodies. This shape gusset may be cut quite separately and joined to the garment in a front and a back seam as in briefs, or may be added to either the front or back of a garment requiring an opening as an extended gusset and become a seam which fastens as in bodies and camiknickers. The gusset may also be divided horizontally through the centre for a seam or an opening, in looser nether garments such as camiknickers or all-in-one pyjamas.

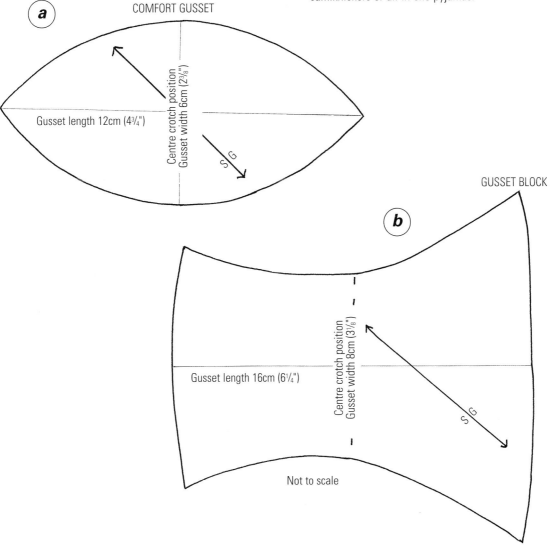

a COMFORT GUSSET

Gusset length 12cm (4³/₄")

Centre crotch position
Gusset width 6cm (2³/₈")

S G

GUSSET BLOCK

b

Gusset length 16cm (6¹/₄")

Centre crotch position
Gusset width 8cm (3¹/₈")

S G

Not to scale

Glossary

Anchor pin	Pin used temporarily to control fabric
Bias	Any direction on fabric which is not the straight grain
Block	Template of body shape: bodice, skirt, sleeve, gusset, etc.
'Body'	All-in-one foundation garment
Body Tolerance	Extra measurement to allow for normal body movement
Bra	Undergarment shaped to cover and support breasts
Bra cup size	A grading from A-G which denotes breast cup size for bras
Briefs	Close-fitting nether undergarment
Bust circle	A circle of 16cm (6¼") diameter centred on the bust point (nipple)
Camisole/ Camiknickers	Woman's underbodice (1894) joined to knickers (1918)
Cummerband	Sash or girdle worn round the waist
Cup divider	Inverted V-shape bent wire to divide the bust cups in bras
Dart manipulation	Moving darts into different positions
Designer ease	Extra fabric to achieve the garment design
Draping	Manipulating fabric into garment designs with elaborate folds
French knickers	Loose nether garment worn next to skin or over foundation
Foundation	Support garment worn next to skin
Lace	Delicate, openwork, netted fabric
Girth	Body measurements at various levels all round the figure
Gusset	An insertion of fabric to allow movement (underarm, crotch etc.,)
Lingerie	Women's undergarments, originally made from linen
Modelling	Manipulating fabric by 'smoothing' into garment shapes
Mules	Open slippers
Negligee	Loose gown worn over nightdress
Pantie	Looser than the close-fitting brief
Pivotting	Keeping a central point stationary whilst rotating a dart
Pyjama	Sleeping suit of loose trousers and jacket (orig. Asian trousers)
Robe	Similar to a dressing gown, to cover undergarments or pyjamas
Shift	Originally a simply-cut undergarment of linen to cover body
Slip	Garment worn under a dress
Suspender belt	Band of fabric holding suspenders to support stockings
Straight grain	Warp (lengthwise) and weft (crosswise) threads in fabric
Stretch fabric	Fabric with elastomeric fibre: extension (stretched); recovery (returned to original state)
Tiered	One or more layers of fabric over another
Thong	Narrow band of fabric to cover the crotch area
Through trunk length	Measurement from nape, between legs to base of front neck
Toile	Trial garment modelled and developed on a dress stand or person
Underwire	Shaped wire inserted in the lower bra cup to support the breasts
Vest	Knitted or woven undergarment (originally an outer garment)
Waspie	Tight-fitting band designed to reduce waist size

Suppliers and further reading

Suppliers

BLOCKS, PATTERNS
AND INFORMATION BOOKLETS

Dawn Cloake
The Fashion Consultancy
P O Box 72, Hayes, Middlesex, UB4 9YZ, UK
Tel/fax: + 44 (020) 8581 3390
email: dawn@cloake73.freeserve.co.uk

BOOKS AND SUPPLIES
R.D. Franks Ltd
Kent House, Market Place, London W1N 8EJ
Tel: + 44 (020) 7636 1244
Fax: + 44 (020) 7436 4904

DRESS STANDS
Kennett and Lindsell Ltd.
Crow Lane, Romford,
Essex RM7 OES, UK
Tel: + 44 (0) 708 749732
Fax: + 44 (0) 708 733328
Telex: 8955855 Kenlin
Cables: Kenlin Romford

MORPLAN
56 Great Titchfield Street
London W1P 8DX
Tel: + 44 (0) 800 435 333
Fax: + 44 (0) 800 451 928

FABRICS & HABERDASHERY
James Hare Silks
Monarch House, P O Box 72
Queen Street, Leeds LS1 1LX, UK

McCulloch & Wallis Ltd
PO Box 3AX
25-26 Dering Street, London W1A 3AX
Tel: + 44 (020) 7409 0725
Fax: + 44 (020) 7491 9578

FASTENERS, INCLUDING 'SNAP-ALLS'
Yale Hook & Eye Company, Inc.,
380 Jelliff Avenue Newark, N.J. 07108 USA
Tel: (201) 824 - 1440,Fax: (201) 824 -3136
& 37 St Michael's Avenue, Stockport
Cheshire SK7 2PW, UK

Michael Daly Fabrics
14-18 St. Mary's Gate, The Lace Market
Nottingham NG1 1PF, UK

Further Reading

Dawn Cloake
FASHION DESIGN ON THE STAND
An introduction to the art of modelling fabric
directly onto the dress stand.
B. T. Batsford Ltd., London, 1996

Dawn Cloake
CUTTING AND DRAPING SPECIAL
OCCASION CLOTHES
Flat pattern cutting and draping techniques
for partywear.
B. T. Batsford Ltd., London, 1998

Helen Stanley
MODELLING AND FLAT CUTTING FOR FASHION
Hutchinson Education Ltd, London, 1983

Ann Haggar
PATTERN CUTTING FOR LINGERIE
Beachwear and Leisurewear.
BSP Professional Books, London

Martin M Shoben & Janet P Ward
PATTERN CUTTING & MAKING UP
Heinemann, London, 1987

Index

Arm: padded 90, 91

Armhole: circumference 22, 23

Asymetric styling: 24, 63, 86

Blocks: bra 92; gussets 93; nether 7;
padded arm, 90, 91

Bodies: 40, 41; evening body 82

Body tolerance: main size chart 12-13;
dress stand 17

Boning: 39, 83, 84

Bras: darted 32, 33; determining cup size 29; bras with cup
seams 34, 35; lace bras 36, 37; long line 38; strapless 39;
halter neck straps 39; taping stand 22, 23;
bra accessories 14, 15

Bra slip: 54

Briefs: 46, 47

Bust: cup divider 15; bust circle 31; separation 30

Bustier: eveningwear 84

Camiknickers: 57

Camisoles: 50, 51, 56; for evening 87

Corselette: 44

Corset: 44; pantie girdle (support pants) 40, 41, 44; for
eveningwear (bustier) 84

Crop tops: 79, 85

Crotchline: measuring depth of 10, 11

Culotte slip: 58; culotte pant combination 58

Curves: modelling, grapefruit exercise 26, 27

Ease: sewing ease 17, 18; designer ease 17, 18

Equipment: 6, 7

Fabrics: 14, 15, 16; straight grain, bias 25; stretch 38, 60

Flare: in half slips 58, 59; in nightdresses 63, 65, 69;
in pyjama tops 78; in ruffles 68, 70

Foundationwear: *see* bodies, bras, corselette, corset,
suspender belt

Gathers: in neck ruffles 68, 70; in knickers 48, 49

Grapefruit exercise: 26, 27

Gussets, in bodies and camiknickers: 40, 42, 43, 46, 47,
48, 49, 82; in camiknickers 57

Half slips: straight half slip 58; flared from yoke 59; pants
combination 58, 88

Knickers: French knickers 46, 48, 49, 63

Lace: applied decoration 54;
edgings and motifs 55; stretch lace 61, 84

Lingerie: stands 9, 11, 19; fasteners 82

Measurements, standard charts
(imperial and metric) 12, 13; taking measurements 10, 11;
standard and individual 19; padded arm 90

Mules: 80, 81

Nether region block: 7

Negligees: 66, 67; for evening 88

Nightshift: 86

Nightwear: 60-81; nightdresses 60-65; tucked and lace 62;
two-tier top 63; floating point nightdress 64, 65; stretch-
lace bodice 61; pyjamas 71-79; robes 68, 69;
designs 79

Pleats: in playsuit pyjamas 77

Pyjamas: 71; all-in-one pyjama 77; pyjama tops 72

Robe: raglan sleeve 68, 69; shortie robe 78

Ruffles: gathered and ungathered 70

Shift: *see* slips, nightshift

Size charts: main 12,13; bust cup 29;
personal record chart 17

Sleepwear: *see* Nightwear

Sleeves: dropped shoulder 78 , kimono 74, 75; raglan 68, 69;
separate 84

Slips: 51, 52, 53, 54; half slips 58; flared from yoke 59; bra
slip 54; culotte slip 58; classic slip 52, 53;
evening shift 86

Stands: 8, 9; padding 20, 21; taping 22, 23; adjustment for
tight fit 30

Stockings: ankle length for evening 89

Strapless: *see* bras

Strap front openings: 72, 73; in a slash 76;
mock strap 72, 76, 77

Suspenders: belt 44

Taping the stand: 22, 23; armhole 23; design lines 24

Tights: 45; for evening 89

Thong: 46

Tightening bust circle: 30, 31

Tolerance: body movement 17,18,19, 20;
reduction 30, 31; design ease, 18; in measurement charts
12, 13; in nightwear 60;
in pyjama trousers 71, 77

Trueing up: 28

Tubular stretch fabric: in stockings 89

Underwear: 29-59; as eveningwear 82-89

Underwires: 15

Vests: 50; for evening - little black vest 85; metallic vest 85;
crop top 79, 85

Waspie: 44; evening waspie 83; laced waspie 83

Yokes: in half-slip 59 ; playsuit pyjama 77